On Earth As It Is In
HEAVEN
A Personal Allegory

Julie Castro

On Earth as It Is in Heaven, A Personal Allegory

Copyright © 2015 by Julie Castro

All rights reserved. No part of this book may be reproduced in any written, electronic, recording, or photocopying form without written permission of the publisher.

ISBN: 978-0-9643613-7-9

10 9 8 7 6 5 4 3 2 1

Printed in the United States of America

Library of Congress Control Number: 2014952993

Scripture quotations taken from the New American Standard Bible®, © 1960, 1962, 1963, 1968, 1971, 1972, 1973, 1975, 1977, 1995 by The Lockman Foundation. Used with permission. (Lockman.org)

Scripture quotations marked NLT are taken from the Holy Bible, New Living Translation, copyright 1996. Used with the permission of Tyndale House Publishers, Inc., Wheaton, Illinois 60189. All rights reserved.

Scripture quotations marked NIV® are taken from the Holy Bible, New International Version ®. Copyright © 1973, 1978, 1984, 2011 by Biblica, Inc. ®. Used with permission. All rights reserved worldwide.

Scripture quotations marked (GNT) are from the Good News Translation in Today's English Version- Second Edition Copyright © 1992 by American Bible Society. Used by Permission.

Scripture taken from the New King James Version®. © 1982 by Thomas Nelson. Used with permission. All rights reserved.

"The Trumpet" and "Small Straws in a Soft Wind" prophetic quotations are taken from the Spirit of Prophecy Bulletin and used with the permission of Faith Tabernacle.

The author has tried to recreate events, locales, and conversations from her memories. In order to maintain anonymity in all instances, the names of all individuals have been changed, with the exception of the author's son.

Editing by: Laura Orsini, Write | Market | Design
Original Cover Artwork by: Lucy C. Flores
Interior and Cover Design by: InfiniteReach Agency

Fiesta Publishing
Phoenix, Arizona
Fiestapublishing.com

To Mac and Mick

CONTENTS

Foreword
1. Introduction 3
2. My First Marriage 5
3. Counterfeits 13
4. Identity and Destiny 19
5. Prophetic Words 23
6. God Speaks to Me Directly 31
7. Following the Instructions 35
8. Confirmations 41
9. Prayer for the Pastor's Wife 51
10. Waiting 55
11. Family and Friends 61
12. The Power of Place 67
13. Exposing Character Flaws 75
14. Hindrances and Deliverances 83
15. One Final Instruction 93
16. Lessons Learned – Great Messages 101
17. Correction and Conviction, but No Condemnation 107
18. Trials and Tribulations 113
19. Doubt 119
20. Reward 123
21. Ministry 127
22. Visions and Dreams 131
23. Season of Waiting 135
24. Symbolic Gestures 143
25. Enjoy This Time with Your Son 147
26. Healing – Stay in the Process 153
27. Personal Victories 161
28. It Was a Test 167

29. Tears	173
30. Trust God	177
31. My Setback Was a Setup	183
32. The Handshake – Betrayal to Promotion	187
33. Suddenly	193
34. Spiritual Reality	197
35. Understanding the Call to Ministry	201
36. God's Will vs. Free Will	205
37. Forgiveness	211
38. The Personal Allegory	217
39. Reflection	219
40. Salvation	221
Acknowledgements	

Foreword

This personal allegory is unlike any other book. It is not commercial or predictable by book publishing standards, but neither is God (also known as Yahweh in the Hebrew language). A price cannot be placed on His commercial viability and His unconventional ways. It is a testimony, a *reality book*, telling the story of a personal journey over a specific period of time. Yet each chapter stands alone, containing a message that is relevant to the bigger picture and overarching theme.

And looking at them Jesus said to them, "With people this is impossible, but with God all things are possible."
Matthew 19:26

CHAPTER 1
Introduction

After graduating from the University of Arizona in Tucson in 1982, I moved to Dallas without a job and only a temporary place to live. It was my first *faith walk*, though I didn't know it at the time. While living in Dallas, I was led to the Lord by my formerly gay roommate in 1985. God raised me up quickly and my walk began at a nondenominational Bible church. Within six weeks, I moved to a Messianic congregation and ultimately landed at a Spirit-filled church. Having lost my job shortly after being saved, I remained at the Spirit-filled church until I moved to San Francisco in 1986. Before the move, I spent the next five months seeking God's face all day long. I lived by Matthew 6:33:

> But seek first His kingdom and His righteousness, and all these things will be added to you.

In San Francisco, I attended an Assembly of God church until God moved me to Hawaii in 1989. While in Hawaii, I visited a few churches, but none of them felt right: the Holy Spirit was missing for me. Returning to Tucson in 1990, I sought God's face, read the Word and prayed, but never attended church. Each city to which God sent me had a specific purpose, and I was in His will, with the exception of being married. Between the time I left Hawaii until I was invited to visit a church in Phoenix, twenty-two years passed; it was my wilderness.

Now living in Phoenix, it wasn't until I attended a going away party for a colleague and friend that I met Mama. My friend introduced her to me, and she gave me a business card for a church. In that moment, the Holy Spirit spoke to me. I knew this would be my new church home. I remember Mama telling me that her son was the pastor, and then asking me if I would like to attend that evening's service with her. I graciously declined, but told her I would visit the following Tuesday.

The presence of the Lord filled the church during the service; it was like the church I had attended in Dallas. I knew this was the church that God wanted me to attend. After service, Mama introduced me to her son, the Pastor. Looking into his eyes, I thought to myself, "Oh no," as something stirred within. In his eyes I saw, *Not another woman my mom is introducing me to!* It was early March and I spent the next five years attending the church faithfully, until God released me.

During the first few years, I went to church on Saturday night and occasionally on Tuesday, but never on Sunday. I loved worshipping the Lord, hearing the Word, and being united with others in God's presence (corporately). I went to church, kept to myself, and left just as quietly. Very rarely did I even shake the pastor's hand; in fact, I generally steered clear of him. But one Sunday morning, the chaplain spoke one prophetic word that changed my whole life and the direction God would take me. It had to do with a future husband. Having had the wrong husband once, I sure didn't want to repeat that mistake again.

This is my testimony of the processes, instructions, lessons, revelations and confirmations that God used to bring me to my destiny.

CHAPTER 2

My First Marriage

In the early 1990s I met a man, a Mexican national from Nogales, Sonora, through mutual acquaintances, a husband and wife, who were believers in Christ. The woman shared a word about me marrying the man, and after three months of testing what she said, I told the Lord, "I want to marry him." God answered my request. It wasn't a prayer, as in asking in the name of Jesus; it was a statement that turned out to be a bad idea, but one that God answered nonetheless. Was the comment my free will? Did I put my will ahead of God's? Was it God's plan for me? Not one to ask questions of Him, I don't have the answer to this day, except to know that it was part of the bigger picture and my destiny.

This was my first lesson about doing things God's way, as opposed to my way. It was a difficult lesson that took twelve years to learn. Instead of trusting God and listening to the guidance He offered through others, I forged ahead and married a man who was never supposed to be my husband.

Three months after meeting him, he wanted to sleep with me. I said, "No. You must marry me if you want to sleep with me." He had been aware that I was a Christian from our first meeting. He would ask about sex, but he never pressured me. He eventually said yes to marriage. I suppose that in my response to him, I had proposed, but in his mind he was only marrying me so he could sleep with me, as no more than a joke, really. Little did I know what I would learn and experience over the next twelve years of marriage. Trusting God in all situations! This was part of my wilderness time.

Before we were married, I asked God to show me this man's heart, and it was pure gold. Seeing his heart in the Spirit, I wanted him as my husband. His compassion for others was incredible. As a medical doctor in Mexico, he worked helping *his people* with free medical care on a regular basis. He gave money to people who didn't have it and offered to help whenever possible. Unfortunately, I would soon find that his compassion toward me was not the same as it was for others. In fact, I rarely experienced compassion or love from him.

After meeting in Nogales, Sonora, we spent weekends together in Tucson, where I lived and owned a home. I neither drank nor smoked, and although he drank beer and smoked cigarettes, I overlooked those nasty habits. I will never forget introducing him to my parents for the first time. He had a cigarette in one hand and a beer in the other. Needless to say, my medical doctor did not make a good impression. Not only did my parents dislike him, but once I announced that we were planning to marry, my sister and sister-in-law came to visit me to try to dissuade me from marrying him. Proverbs 12:15 states:

> The way of a fool is right in his own eyes, but a wise man is he who listens to counsel.

I didn't listen.

We were married by a justice of the peace in Tucson, but no one knew. I got pregnant immediately, and we were married before the Lord by a local pastor a few months later. The first indication that I should have never married him was the day he tried to burn the marriage license. He was so angry with me for some reason that I don't even remember, yet I ignored his anger. Red flags were everywhere, but I continued to ignore them. I brought to the marriage a house in Tucson, furniture, jewelry, and a sports car. When I met and married him, he was not working as a medical doctor, even though he had a medical degree which allowed him to work throughout the entire country of Mexico. Along with not working, he only owned the clothes on his back – a shirt, jeans, underwear, and flip-flops. He had been married before and, unfortunately, preferred not to pay child support for his son, so he chose not to work.

Before we were married, he had lived with his mother in a house without a bathroom. The only running water was the garden hose connected to the house. The toilet was a bucket behind the house, very primitive compared to U.S. standards. When I visited Mexico, he always took me to one of his friends' homes to use the restroom and shower. This standard of living was far lower than I had ever experienced, but I never passed judgment. I never complained and I always loved his mom, his half-sister, and her children.

Shortly before I moved to Nogales, Sonora, to live with him, he got a job with Sonora's social medicine system. He earned $635 a month as a doctor and worked in a pharmacy on the side to make ends meet. My husband worked ten-hour days while I raised our son, read the Word, prayed, and sang praises during the day.

He was a very well-known doctor because of his compassion and his "connections," and everyone knew he had married a *blondie*, an American. He preferred the less fortunate as his friends, as he felt more comfortable with them than with the wealthy, although he spent time with other professionals – doctors, dentists, and attorneys – for business purposes. Those so-called friends who were less fortunate – the afflicted and addicted – had the mistaken impression that since he was a doctor who was married to an American, we had money. In their eyes, if they stole something, it didn't matter because we could easily replace it. They stole everything we owned, at one point or another, within the first two years of our marriage.

Through it all, God was with me, proving Himself again and again. I was standing on the His Word, even though my husband was not a believer. Raised Catholic, he knew Jesus in his head, but not in his heart. He did not have the personal relationship with the Lord that I did.

They said, "Believe in the Lord Jesus, and you will be saved, you and your household. Acts 16:31

Over time, everything that was stolen was restored. Cases in point: my jewelry and convertible sports car were stolen within the first six months of my living in Mexico. It took a few years, but both the car and jewelry were restored after we moved to Tucson, better than those that were stolen. Zephaniah 3:20 states:

> *"At that time I will bring you in, even at the time when I gather you together; Indeed, I will give you renown and praise among all the peoples of the earth, when I restore your fortunes before your eyes," says the LORD.*

It was a testimony to show others that God is a God of restoration.

When the peso devalued, my husband decided he wanted to immigrate to the U.S. I applied to Immigration and Naturalization Services on his behalf, and ten months later he had his Green Card. We moved into my house and started our life in America. During the early years of our marriage, my husband continually told me he married me as a joke and that we needed to get divorced. I persevered, but after about two years of hearing that he had married me as a joke, I'd had enough. It was starting to take a toll on me. Proverbs 18:21 says:

> *Death and life are in the power of the tongue, and those who love it will eat its fruit.*

I was experiencing a slow death. When I finally agreed to the divorce, he changed his mind. He had become accustomed to the American life style – a house, two cars, travel, disposable income, and a lot of entertaining.

My husband felt that being Mexican meant he could be *macho* and stay out all night with his married male friends. I began to pray, and although it took two years, he eventually saw that he was about to lose the *good life* when he found a garbage bag outside the house filled with all of his belongings. It contained far more than he had brought to the marriage. This was a wakeup call, and over time he changed, but not without a lot of fervent prayer and speaking the Word of God to him.

There were good years, but overall it was a marriage that should have never taken place. What came out of it was an incredible son, Manuel, which means *God with us*. My husband chose the name, after the father he had never known. Known as Mac, our son was a huge blessing to both of us, and he was appropriately named!

Before Manuel was born, I prayed and asked the following: that the Spirit of the Lord would be with my child. When people came in contact with my baby, the presence of Jesus would be obvious and people were naturally drawn to the child. Little did I know the profound effect of the prayer for my child in utero; to this day, people are naturally drawn to Mac.

As my husband's income increased, so did his beer and cocaine consumption. Our family's needs were always met, but he felt entitled to spend his share of the disposable income that resulted from our modest lifestyle on his *entertainment*. Part of the family's entertainment included dining out frequently, as I didn't cook and that way everyone could eat what they wanted.

At year ten of the marriage, I was at the end of my rope. The drugs, alcohol, and verbal abuse were wearing me down. If I had not had Jesus, things would have been much worse. But thank the Lord, God sticks to you more closely than any friend. He was right by my side as I experienced daily life with my husband. I finally cried out to the Lord and asked to be released. I still remember, to this day, standing in the hallway holding on to the foosball table and crying out, "Please God, let me out of this marriage!" It was two more years before it happened.

The release came the day my husband greeted me at the door as I was leaving to drive Mac to school before work. He was all coked up, and began telling me in Spanish that he was going to rip my face apart. I looked at him, walked past him out the door, and got in the car. If the devil was trying to put fear in me, it didn't work! As I started the engine, Mac said, "Mom, that was scary. I thought you were going to get a divorce."

I looked at my son and answered him, "Mac, he is your father, but I have stayed in this marriage far too long. Now that you have said this, I will file for divorce."

It is amazing how God works when you let Him. During the two years after crying out to the Lord, God gave my husband many chances to repent and get things right. Continually, God would give me prophetic words to speak to him, but each time, he refused to listen. Then, in one moment, God opened the door for my divorce, using my son's words to release me from the marriage.

* * *

At that time, I was the director of a nonprofit agency that helped women with barriers to employment get back into the workforce. Since the program was housed within a university, an Advisory Board was in place, rather than a Board of Directors. The day my husband threatened me, I had an Advisory Board meeting. One look at my face, and my fellow board members knew something was wrong. I confided to them that I needed to get out of my marriage but was unable to afford an attorney. One of the board members, a retired Superior Court Judge, told me she would call in a favor.

That favor resulted in one of the most prominent divorce attorneys in Tucson taking my case, pro bono. It took about a month before we met face to face, but the paperwork was filed in June and my husband was served with divorce papers shortly thereafter. When the process server presented him with the papers, he tore the documents up in front of the woman. My husband didn't want the divorce, but he didn't have the money to hire an attorney to contest it, so my divorce was decreed sixty-nine days after the papers were filed.

I received full custody of our son. I didn't ask for any alimony or child support, as I was certain I wouldn't get it. I felt it was better not to make the request so that my son would never have to ask why his dad hadn't helped me financially. He had never paid child support to his first wife for my step-son, so why would things change for *our* son. I did not want my son to have a deadbeat dad.

It was August when my divorce was finalized. I remember standing in the computer room and saying out loud, "Lord, it is OK with me if I never marry again." He answered my spirit, and I knew that one day I would again be married, but the next time it would be to a believer in Jesus. I had no idea how short or long a time I would have to wait, but I knew I would get married again.

By the following February, my ex-husband had begun stalking me. The cocaine paranoia had kicked in, and he was convinced there was another man in my life. Not that that should have affected him, as we were now divorced. He would show up at my house at all hours of the day and night, and sometimes barge right in. One evening I called the police, and later that night he was arrested and thrown in jail. First thing the next morning, I was at City Court filing a restraining order of protection for my son and myself.

I knew I needed to move. And coincidentally, my dad shared with me at dinner one night that he'd had a dream that I moved to another city. This was the opportunity to explain to my parents that my ex was stalking me and I needed to move. Five weeks after filing the restraining order, I found a job in Phoenix, sold my house in Tucson, and bought one in Phoenix. It was now May, nine months following the divorce. Just as quickly as God granted my divorce, He made the move a reality. Little did I know that the move was the beginning of other journeys that would place me on the path to my destiny, experiences that were both painful and joyous.

It has been at least five years since I have seen my ex-husband. He has called a few times over the years to talk about reconciliation, and has sent text messages. I responded only on a few occasions. The first incident began with a phone call late at night that caught me off-guard. He wanted to talk, I stalled by responding, "We'll see." About a week later, I received three text messages. The first advised that if I didn't want to talk, I should just say so. I texted back: *There is no reason to talk unless it has to do with Manuel. And he is fine.* Then he texted: *Are you married or what?* I didn't respond. A few minutes later he texted: *I still love you.* Again, I didn't respond. I knew in the moment after receiving these text messages that the door was closed and could not be reopened, even though he still occasionally tries. Thank you, Jesus.

Although I don't live under the law, but under grace, I have often wondered if Numbers 30:5 applies to me.

> *But if her father should forbid her on the day he hears of it, none of her vows or her obligations by which she has bound herself shall stand; and the LORD will forgive her because her father had forbidden her.*

I went into my first marriage in haste, and my dad never approved of it. Am I forgiven? And in God's eyes, was I even married?

Undeniably, His favor is with me, even in my mistake of marrying the wrong man. During the twelve years of my marriage, I relied on God for my strength, direction, joy, and identity. It has been nine years since my divorce, and what God has done over the last three years is a testimony no one can deny. God has His hand on me and can now do what He wants regarding the husband and marriage that *will be.*

The wilderness of not attending church and being married was all preparation for my future.

CHAPTER 3
Counterfeits

The enemy will often send a counterfeit – someone who seems like the real deal, though they are not. The purpose is to detour us from God's path for us. In hindsight, the doctor was not supposed to be my husband; but what the enemy intended as an instrument of evil, God used to further the good in both of us. Though my ex-husband was a counterfeit and our marriage may have delayed my destiny, God will accomplish what He has prepared for each of us if we will only do His will, not our own. This was true in my case, but I didn't realize it until a gentleman friend came into my life.

Being ever faithful, God will get us back on track. The key is for us to get back on track quickly: learn the lessons, accept the discipline, and move forward, knowing God has each of us in His hand. Had I known about counterfeits, it would have saved me a great deal of heartache, but I believe that my heartache will enable me to help someone else, going forward.

While working as director of the community-based organization, I was the only person outside of Maricopa County appointed to participate in a special taskforce. Since my career at that point focused on workforce development, I was assigned to the appropriate subcommittee. The first couple of meetings I attended, the name of a man was mentioned regularly, as he was a key member of the subcommittee. He eventually became the person God used to plant the seed in my mind about moving to Phoenix. Though I was still unaware of it, God already knew I would be getting divorced and would need to move quickly.

God had His hand on me in that situation, as this man continued to suggest, even while I still lived in Tucson, that I should to move to Phoenix. At first, it wasn't even a consideration. Months later, I began to entertain the idea, *Maybe, once Mac graduates from high school, in about eight years.* Then I considered a two-year window. Having driven and attended various work-related meetings in Phoenix, I was accustomed to the area and knew a lot of people there who were also working for nonprofit organizations. But it would not be until several months after my divorce, when I had to move for the safety of my son and myself, that our move to Phoenix became a reality.

It was August when I finally put a name and face together for this man. The day I was finally introduced to him, he asked for my business card. About a week later he called and asked if I would like to have dinner with him after an upcoming meeting. I was shocked, and asked him, "What would I tell my son?"

He responded, "What does your son have to do with anything?"

"My divorce isn't final yet," I explained.

He quickly informed me that he, too, was in the process of a divorce. I was surprised, because he'd been wearing a wedding band when I met him. I accepted his invitation and noticed that his wedding ring was absent on the day we met for dinner. I questioned him extensively about his divorce. He told me that it was proving to be a slow, nasty process, in large part because of his wealth. Nine days after we had dinner for the first time, my divorce was final.

That dinner would be the first of many over the next six years. He became my gentleman friend and during those years, he was in and out of my life. We would have dinner two or three times a month, but then when he felt he was getting too close to me, he would flee. The first time he stopped calling was about a year after our initial dinner. A spirit of rejection surrounded him, which manifested itself by involving women and then cutting them off. My awareness of this spirit came after a few months of conversations, actions and observations between me, my gentleman friend, and others who worked in the same field and attended the same meetings. For whatever reason, however, when he would cut himself off from me, he would return within the year. During some of those cutoff years, we did meet, but rarely.

I think he felt the love and compassion that God gave me for him and desired it. He was a believer, but not necessarily a committed one. When he would call after having disappeared for a period of time, I would let him back into my life. Not only did I enjoy his mind and his friendship, but I was also moved by showing love to a person who never experienced unconditional love before. I truly believed God was using me to break down some strongholds in his life and heal some of his past hurts.

Eventually, Mr. Smith started going back to church. I spoke with him about how God was moving in my life, and he began to talk more about Jesus as His Lord and Savior. He started reading the Word again, and recognized the Lord's hand on his life from childhood, through Vietnam, and as a successful businessman.

We laughed, learned, and loved. We were two people healing from lifetimes of hurts. God used Mr. Smith to tell me one of the most profound things I have ever heard, which broke my chains of low self-esteem. He said, "Do you know why you are so beautiful? Because you have no idea how beautiful you are." To this day, I reflect on that statement when I find myself questioning my appearance. My dad did a real number on me with his criticism, and it usually had to do with my appearance. The scripture God gave me to stand on was Ezekiel 16:14:

> "Then your fame went forth among the nations on account of your beauty, for it was perfect because of My splendor which I bestowed on you," declares the Lord GOD.

I needed to hear that I was beautiful, as neither my husband nor any other man had ever said it until my gentleman friend. Walls began to come down.

I continued to fill Mr. Smith with the Word of God and acknowledged how He was moving in my life. And I continued to be forgiving: my gentleman friend would cancel dinner plans, and it was fine; he would walk out for a period of time, and I would let him back into my life. Call me foolish, but he needed to learn that I wasn't going to reject him, even if he rejected me. Isn't that what Jesus did when He died on the cross for us? A few years into our friendship, I started attending the church that Mama had invited me to, and often shared with him how the presence of God moved me.

When I shared with him the prophetic word I'd received regarding *Julie getting a husband,* it was the last time I saw him. With God's grace, that door was now closed. As much as I cared for Mr. Smith, I needed to think about what God had in store for me. Through prayer, I realized nothing was going to happen for me until I released him and moved forward. We had completed the purposes God had intended for each of us, and great healing occurred in me.

God showed me in a dream that Mr. Smith had found another woman and had moved on. I was at peace with that outcome, and He closed the door by giving me Ezekiel 44:2:

> The LORD said to me, "This gate shall be shut; it shall not be opened, and no one shall enter by it, for the LORD God of Israel has entered by it; therefore it shall be shut."

True to character, Mr. Smith tried coming back into my life about a year-and-a-half later, but he never said, "I'm sorry" or "my divorce is final." I was sure this was the enemy, attempting to keep me from my destiny – while at the same time, God began to move in my life. I had to rely completely on His attributes and promises to keep me from falling back into the same pattern. My habitual cycle with Mr. Smith needed to end, so I pressed in and began to thank the Lord for what He was doing in my life and what He was planning for me. Looking back, I realize Mr. Smith's final attempt to come back into my life was the beginning of a fifteen-to seventeen-month ordeal of constant enemy attacks. The devil used friends, colleagues, and members of the church body to try to wear me down. I had never experienced anything like it before, but now I feel prepared if it should happen again.

I continued to pray for him, even though he was not a part of my life. A couple years passed and Mr. Smith was heavy on my heart. I was asking the Lord whether or not I should contact him; around the same time a prophet told me that people will support my upcoming ministry, financially. This was a confirmation, but I needed another one. The second one came the next day via a prophetic listserv to which I subscribe. The message was:

> *Take time to reconnect with some of those that you have lost touch with. I will lead you by way of remembrance and give you a desire to communicate. You can now bridge the gap that has been created through time and circumstances. Don't be afraid to let others know that you care about them, says the Lord.*
> "Small Straws in a Soft Wind" by Marsha Burns, Faith Tabernacle

Confirmations presented, God opened the door for Mr. Smith to return to my life for three-and-a-half hours. This time, I was well on the road to my destiny. Having listened to the story of what God was doing in my life, Mr. Smith was amazed at what he heard. I was the one to contact him, and perhaps he thought things would be like they had been in the past – but they weren't. If it was God's will, I was open to being friends, even though he still was not divorced. I received a text from him the next day: *Had a gr8 time. Let's get together again.*

I texted back, *Yes, it was fun. I look forward to it. Next time you are in town on a Sunday I hope to see you in church.* It wasn't until a few months later that I received a reply.

This had been a test, and I passed. I still don't understand why God allowed that last meeting to take place. Maybe it was for my gentleman friend, and not even about me. At a prayer meeting, I requested to understand the purpose of our reconnecting. The director of the Prayer

Ministry prayed, from Proverbs 3:5:

> *Trust in the LORD with all your heart And do not lean on your own understanding.*

My imagination has not run wild, and I have been able to release my need to analyze why the meeting took place; this in and of itself is an accomplishment in my growth with the Lord.

Sometimes we are led to do things that aren't about us or our growth, but which happen for the betterment of the other person.

CHAPTER 4

Identity and Destiny

The lesson about counterfeits was finished, now God started to show me my identity and destiny. From a young age, I knew I was different from others, in terms of the way I dressed, my confidence, and my life experiences. Although I have a lot of friends, I never really *fit in* anywhere. An introvert by nature, I am very happy staying home, reading the Word, praying, and spending time with the Lord. I don't need to be entertained! Quite content with my life, I was surprised when, unexpectedly and later in life, God began to show me who He was calling me to be. Just one more point that sets me apart for His glory.

The lesson? Don't limit yourself! Let God establish and guide you to become the person He has called you to be. He will use others and circumstances to catapult you into that place of being; allow them into your life. In my case, God used guest speakers at church to bring me into the realization of who I am in Christ. 2013 was a significant year, and March was particularly notable, as it is my birth month and God used this appointed time to *birth* new revelations in me. Details I knew about myself to some extent were now coming into their fullness after many years of being hidden.

Perhaps the most significant revelation was understanding the call on my life that happened when I was seven years old. At the time, I had no idea of this episode's significance. I was raised Catholic and was preparing to participate in my *first communion*. The priests and nuns asked all the little girls' parents to dress them in any color other than white; they didn't want the girls looking like milk bottles, according to my mom. Having been raised Protestant, she was ecstatic about this request and eager to comply.

This is my duck, duck, goose story.

A line of more than one hundred little girls were ready to walk down the church aisle, all dressed in white. Duck, duck, duck, *goose*... There I walked, dressed in a canary yellow dress with matching canary yellow patent leather shoes – the only girl whose mom followed the request, the only one who dressed accordingly, who was not wearing a white dress. Duck, duck...

I remember receiving many compliments from the priests and nuns, and as much as I loved the dress and shoes, I stood apart from all the other little girls. Sometime in my late 30s or early 40s, I reflected on that first communion, when God had shown me that I was different from others. The memory of this event was always with me, but it wasn't until I recounted the story to a first-time visitor to the church, that I had full revelation of the event. As I shared the story, God spoke to me and said, "I called you when you were seven years old." I began to cry. Until now, I'd never understood. I had been set apart for such a time as this, and it was my mother's obedience to the Lord that led to the beginning of my destiny, a calling I would not fully discover until more than forty-five years later.

God asks that we love our neighbor as we love ourselves (Matthew 22:39). Again in the same month, I had an epiphany and understood the Lord's call as an intercessor in my life. It was a visiting local pastor who was ministering at church for the weekend and so eloquently said, "You know you are a true intercessor when you can forgive quickly." I realized in that moment that God had given me the gift of forgiveness. Jesus is the first and true Intercessor, but God blessed me with a forgiving heart and the ability to not take offense from others when they speak or act poorly toward me. I now believe that is why I was able to stay in a bad marriage for twelve years and be a friend to a hurting man.

However, it was the words preached by a female pastor from California who came to minister at a women's ministry meeting that would have the most profound effect on my life. The message – *Identity and Destiny*. I had already received many prophetic words and confirmations regarding my identity and future as a pastor's wife, but I was a long way from walking that path.

The process concerning my purpose wasn't yet making any sense to me, but a year later when the *Identity and Destiny* CD kept showing up in my car, I took notice and began to listen to it. What I heard was an explanation of everything that God had taken me through over the past year. I couldn't believe it. I now understood the purpose – hurts healed, soul ties broken, character flaws addressed, all while walking in faith and waiting for God. I now had an overall understanding of how God had brought me to the place I needed to be in order to become a pastor's wife and operate in full-time ministry. God gave this pastor a word as we praised and worshiped, and she shared it with the women:

> "Let me develop my love and character in you. Do not go out premature. Allow me to cultivate that which is inside of you."

> She then stated the following, as further explanation. "Don't quit, don't give in. Don't go ahead of God and don't stay too far behind. Walk with Him. If it's not happening on your time table, don't quit. Don't give up. Just keep waiting."

One Saturday night, the Lord spoke to me and said, "It's big – be humble." At the time, I had no idea what the message meant, but as time passed and prophetic words and confirmations were spoken by ministry leaders to me, my identity became clearer, my mission defined; it was more than being a wife and it was bigger than a women's ministry. I was called to be a spokeswoman for the Lord God Almighty, Himself, with a specific assignment. As it says in Jeremiah 1:5:

> *Before I formed you in the womb I knew you, And before you were born I consecrated you; I have appointed you a prophet to the nations.*

CHAPTER 5

Prophetic Words

Prophecy is defined as an utterance or revelation inspired by God and the Holy Spirit that foretells or predicts what is to come. Prophetic words can be spoken by anyone, as prophecy is a gift from God. 2 Peter 1:21 says:

> *for no prophecy was ever made by an act of human will, but men moved by the Holy Spirit spoke from God.*

Sometimes prophetic words are spoken by a person who is unaware that they are speaking prophetically. Other times, someone may get a word of knowledge while praying for another. Prophecies are also spoken to the church, or Body of Christ.

Test the word that is being spoken. Does it line up with the Word of God? Does it confirm what the Holy Spirit has already spoken, or is it a word that releases you into your destiny? 1 Corinthians 14:22 states:

> *So then tongues are for a sign, not to those who believe but to unbelievers; but prophecy is for a sign, not to unbelievers but to those who believe.*

I believe in prophetic words, but I am also cautious. Does the person speaking the word have a proven track record of speaking under the unction of the Holy Spirit?

Be wary of those who speak words that aren't in line with the Word of God. Known as false prophets, these *parking lot prophets* draw upon their own inspiration to speak false words into a person's life. Often, the words tickle the listener's ear in order to gain favor with him or her. Or, they may be tapping into familiar spirits which are not of God.

Many times in the Old Testament, especially in the book of Jeremiah, prophets would speak what they believed the kings wanted to hear, as opposed to the truth. But Jeremiah, the prophet who followed God's instructions, spoke as commanded, knowing the words were usually chastisement or detrimental to the people and would often land him in a cistern or prison cell.

I have had only a handful of prophetic words spoken into my life, and most of them came through guest speakers at church. Each spoken word either released me into my destiny or confirmed what I already knew.

> But when my servant makes a prediction, when I send a messenger to reveal my plans, I make those plans and predictions come true... Isaiah 44:26 (GNT)

The first prophetic word spoken over me was by a local pastor. I knew he had a word for me and when the invitation to the congregation to go up to the altar for prayer was announced, I accepted. When the visiting pastor came to me, he blessed me and began to walk away – but then he returned and spoke. All I remember him saying was, "Untapped potential." I knew this was true. Helping others get back into the workforce had been my profession while I lived in Tucson, and I now wanted to help the unemployed people in the congregation. As a result, I sent the church pastor a note offering my services to conduct job readiness workshops. I think that was the first note I ever sent the pastor, but I was never taken up on my offer.

It was a few years later when the most profoundly prophetic word was spoken. The pastor mentioned in earlier services that the chaplain would be preaching on Sunday. I was going to be in Tucson, but the Lord spoke to me, saying, "I have a word for you." At the end of his message the *word* went forth. He called my name; and as far as I knew, I was the only Julie at the church. This word, spoken by the chaplain, was:

Julie, I have just what you need; and I need you to simply follow my instructions. Stop trying to do it your way. You'll never get a husband. Just do it My way, because if you continue to do it your way, you're going to get a husband, but it's not the one you're supposed to have.

It was a few weeks before a friend gave me a copy of the prophetic message from that Sunday service. This word was the catalyst for all the instructions, confirmations, and processes that I would brave over the next three years. When I listened to it, I was shocked. I didn't know what to make of the message, but as I listened, I carefully wrote it down. It wasn't an encouraging word; in fact, it had an element of discipline: I had been doing it my way, not His way. My gentleman friend was my way. The pastor, it would turn out, would be His way. The interesting thing is that long before I heard that prophetic word, I said to my gentleman friend, "I don't know if it's you or the pastor, but I believe one of you two may be my husband."

Having forgotten about the prophetic word, a few months passed before I read it again. This time, I read it with a new perspective, realizing I had been receiving instructions from the Lord. Again, I was in shock, as the prophetic words were now beginning to make sense. The chaplain's message would be the foundation for many of the words regarding my destiny.

Each time I reread the prophetic message it led to a better understanding of what I was experiencing in my daily walk with the Lord. The biggest revelation of *doing it my way* had to do with my efforts to get my gentleman friend to finalize his divorce. When I realized I was trying to control the situation, rather than trusting God to work on my behalf, I knew I was not acting according to God's will, and I repented.

In February, the Lord told me to call in sick. I actually came down with a bad stomach ache in the morning, so I stayed home. Led to turn on the TV, I turned the channel to a Christian broadcast. At 7:30 a.m. a man with a well-known international healing ministry program was on the air. Familiar with the ministry, I watched the show. The bottom of the TV screen flashed the dates and times he was to be in Phoenix: he was in town that very day and would be ministering at 10 a.m.! I got ready and went to the church where he was speaking. I saw some people from my church and sat with them.

The Friday morning service was supposed to be on a pre-determined topic, but when the healing pastor began to speak, his topic was the restoration of gifts, something other than what had been planned. I received the scriptures and the information, but what was amazing was that the healing pastor and I stared at each other for a moment, and then my spirit flipped. I knew in that moment, the gift of healing had been imparted and restored to me. The woman sitting next to me acknowledged that she, too, saw it happen in the Spirit. God had restored the gift of healing He'd first bestowed upon me when I was born again in Dallas and walked in while living in San Francisco.

This incident is noteworthy, because the California-based pastor who was in Phoenix for the same healing crusade came to our church services that weekend and ministered on behalf of the pastor, who was under the weather. That Saturday night was the next time a prophetic word was spoken over me. I had been sensing a call to full-time ministry by this time, and when the female pastor gave a call from the altar to those who believed they had been called into ministry, I went forward. But she got sidetracked for a while with a healing anointing; an hour or so later, she began to speak over me. This is what I remember, as it was so profound:

"Woman of God, woman of God. I have seen you reading, studying, and meditating on My Word."

She spoke some more things which I don't remember, and then said, *"There is an explosion on you."*

In that moment, the visiting pastor looked around for our pastor, but he had already left. She said a few more things, and then I went down in the Spirit. I believe the explosion she saw on me was the same one she saw on the pastor when she'd prayed for him earlier in the service.

It wasn't until the following Tuesday, when I shared the words with a friend, that the California pastor's words actually sunk in. I started to cry. Me? A woman of God? I was in shock, to say the least. Such a thing had been the furthest thing from my mind. In June, I sent her a thank you card and an offering for the word she'd spoken over me back in February.

In July of the same year, the California pastor and the co-pastor of her church were in town for the weekend and visited my church for its Tuesday night service. She had written a thank you card and personally handed it to me. I remember her telling me that I reminded me of her, when she first started in the ministry. Then she told me, "Just walk it out." During that same Tuesday service, the co-pastor told me how touched her colleague had been by my note, as she speaks many words into people's lives but rarely hears back from them. As the co-pastor and I talked, she invited me to attend her ministry's eighth anniversary celebration in Beverly Hills, California, coming up that August.

It worked out that I was able to attend the anniversary celebration. I stayed overnight with a friend who lives in Beverly Hills, and we went to the gathering together. The guest speaker for the celebration shared her personal testimony, to which my friend related. At the end of her testimony, she asked if anyone needed prayer. At the encouragement of my friend, I went. The guest speaker asked the need of my prayer request. I responded, "Just pray." I personally prefer not to reveal the details of my life, so I know that the prayer is being led by the Holy Spirit. She began to pray:

Plan. God's plan. You know God's plan for you. I am here to confirm His plan for you.

At that point, I fell in the Spirit, and the woman continued to pray over me. Though I don't know what was said, I believed this was God's plan for me: I would be the pastor's wife and I would be responsible for the women's ministry.

In February, the chaplain preached again. This time, the prophetic word from the pulpit was:

The marriage that should have never been, it is finished; and the marriage that is to be, it is finished.

I started to cry, as I knew the word was for me. A few weeks later, during the monthly women's ministry meeting, I talked to a woman about the prophetic word. I told her I had received the word, and she asked me if I was married. I responded, "No, divorced." We looked at each other, and I knew that she knew about the pastor and me.

She said, "You will be soon." Later she told me that she saw it in the Spirit, but never mentioned the pastor's name. It was later confirmed as she sat next to me the evening the pastor preached Part III of the *Three Gs – Glory, Gold, and Guys & Girls.* She kept nudging me as he spoke about how to know if the person is from the Lord or not. I confirmed her nudges.

In July, I was publically baptized for the first time, after having had a relationship with Jesus for twenty-eight years. I mention this, as a woman said to me, "Since you were baptized, you will experience something that will give you insight into your future." It was an utterance that came to pass three days later. Jesus was crucified, died, buried, and rose again on the third day. Three days after I was publically water baptized, a prophetic word was spoken by the spiritual son of the healing pastor.

The service began, and during the praise and worship I continuously affirmed, "Yes." At one point, the spiritual son turned around and looked at me. I opened my eyes, looked at him, and then I closed my eyes. I believe God was talking to him, and "Yes" was a confirmation. Throughout the evening, he would look at me, but it wasn't until I went up for prayer that another confirmation and prophetic word was spoken over me.

Following God's instructions, I went up for prayer toward the end of the evening. I was one of the last people he prayed over that night. The word spoken was:

You have been called to the nations; the world is your mission field.

This was yet another prophetic word confirming my identity and destiny. The word regarding the nations was similar to the pastor's; he too, has a call to the nations. God wouldn't put two people together as husband and wife if they didn't have the same call on their lives.

The word brought to mind my desire to travel the world. In fact, I had wanted to be a flight attendant in my teens, but at the time, a woman had to be at least twenty years old to work for a major airline. I decided to attend the university for two years, but by the time I turned twenty, I already had two years of schooling behind me, so I continued my education. Upon graduation, I moved to Dallas, the airline's headquarters, but I never applied to become a flight attendant. I reflected and wondered, "Is God now going to fulfill the desire to travel that I had so many years ago?" I looked forward to the prophetic word to come to pass, for Isaiah 42:9 states:

See, the former things have taken place, and new things I declare; before they spring into being I announce them to you. (NIV)

It wasn't until some months later that another prophetic word would be spoken over me. I was invited by the California pastor to attend a different church in Phoenix where she was ministering for the weekend.

The word she spoke was long and full of confirmations. Some of the highlights are:

> ... Julie, promotion is coming. There is something big that God is putting in your hands that nobody knows about, but you. Is that right? (While this was happening, my friends were saying, "So right," and laughing. "So right.") Is it right? It's interesting because it's almost like a gold chip. I don't know what that means, but it carries a lot of weight to glory. It carries a lot of influence. It's a chip. It's a gold chip. The Lord said, it couldn't happen until now. It had to be now.... WOW! You're going to sing a new song. Fulfillment's coming.... It's a chip, it's almost like, I don't know what that means. It's like a computer chip. The California pastor and I said this at the same time.
>
> But it's gold. Yeah, Jesus, I love Jesus.... So Lord, use Julie. Send her out. Send her forth. I see an envelope, too, with like a little chip in it. I don't know what that means, sending out. Wow, that everything You've given her be sent out, may be used and utilized for Your purpose. Protect it. Cover it. Guard it. Anoint it. And bring it forth. In Jesus' name, release it. Release Your glory on Your daughter, **on Your daughter.** Hallelujah!

Then the pastor spoke again, "He said, 'Give them their diplomas right now.' You just graduated, Julie! You just graduated." She went on to give my two friends diplomas, as well. We had all been through some trials, endured the pain, and now had God promoted us to the next level. I understood most of the word, as it was a confirmation of what I already knew, but the comment about the promotion that would take place three weeks later was not something I foresaw.

CHAPTER 6
God Speaks to Me Directly

One night, God gave me a word which I thought was about my gentleman friend and his eminent return. The word was, "The longer you wait, the closer you are to your desire coming to pass." I was led to share this with the pastor one Sunday after church in November. This was the first time I was instructed to share a prophetic word with him, and the word was actually for and about us.

Early in the morning on New Year's Eve day, while visiting my parents, God spoke to me in the early morning. He said, "If you will decrease completely, you can have **ALL** things."

I remember chuckling to myself and saying, "You mean the pastor *and* a five-carat pink sapphire engagement ring." I said these two things because by this time, I had been following through on all kinds of unusual instructions and was beginning to realize the possibility that the pastor was to be my husband. But, I was still running.

Now I had to figure out what needed to decrease completely. After a few days of meditating on God's words to me, a conversation with friend about tithing came to mind. At that point, I wasn't tithing. I was giving to the church, but not the ten percent that God asks of us. With my *first fruit* offering at the New Year's Eve service that night, and going forward, I began tithing and have continued ever since. God has richly blessed me with a lower interest rate and a fifteen-year mortgage on my house, extra money when I needed it, and many other things too numerous to recall or recount.

In August, God started to speak to me shortly after I began a ten-day fast from television. Of the many things He began to speak, He told me to listen to what Pastor was saying from the pulpit. On one occasion, he addressed the idea of *"caught, not taught."* I knew the word was for me, so I began to listen intently to what was being said. One Sunday, the pastor brought a high school football player to everyone's attention. He suggested that people go and support him during his games. I knew I was to go. This was an example of a "caught, not taught" moment.

As a pastor's wife, I knew I would need to get out of my comfort zone and be willing to do things that I wouldn't normally do, like attend a high school football game. I needed to learn how to support church members outside of church. I was the first to arrive at the football stadium and wondered why I was there. Even as others began to arrive, I still felt uncomfortable and out of place.

The pastor saw me, and a look of bewilderment crossed his face, as if he was thinking, "What is *she* doing at the game?" As the evening progressed, I relaxed and became more comfortable. I shared a few details about my son and his studies at the university with one of the other church members who showed up, also following the pastor's suggestion to support the young man on the team. This was the second time he had ever seen me outside of church and the first time at a non-church function. There was more to me than he knew.

At one point, the young man made a touchdown. Pastor became very excited and mentioned to someone in the stands that he was the pastor of the young man who had made the touchdown. He was so proud. I just looked at him and beamed him a huge smile. I turned, and suddenly God's all-consuming fire came upon me. I knew in that moment that something had changed between us. From that point forward, I saw the pastor watching and listening to me from my peripheral vision.

God spoke to me that night and said, "I am going to start to move between the two of you." On Sunday, He moved. While in the greeting line, a woman came up to me and told me that the testimony I had shared at the women's ministry meeting had really blessed her. It produced in her a heart cry for a deeper relationship with Jesus. I prayed for her, and we both began to weep.

Pastor started his message with Jeremiah 1:4-5:

> The word of the LORD came to me, saying, "Before I formed you in the womb I knew you, before you were born I set you apart; I appointed you as a prophet to the nations." (NIV)

I began to cry. This is the scripture I use to describe myself. I have said to friends, "I'm a modern day Jeremiah," as God uses me to speak encouragement, but to also speak reprimands to others. And know, encouraging words are much easier to speak! To this day, I will speak reprimands at His instruction, but I sure don't like doing it. And when God asks me to speak a reprimand, I am usually the last one He sends. I just pray the person gets it right before I am asked to speak anything.

As the pastor preached, he addressed pride. I had been praying against this spirit for him, as I believed pride was hindering him from shaking my hand. As he preached, he said, "Sometimes, the message or the solution doesn't come in the package we expect, and we can miss the blessing if we judge who God uses to send the answer." In that moment, I began to think that maybe I was not who he was expecting as a wife. I was still weeping, not fully understanding why.

At one point during the message, the pastor came over to the section where I was sitting, stretched out his hand, and said, "I am the one you are waiting for." I knew what he was telling me. He was acknowledging himself as my husband, confirming it to me. But he was in the Spirit at the time, and I don't think he really understood what he was saying. I looked at him as I dried my tears. It was then that I realized I was in travail, so I leaned over to the woman next to me and told her, as she had seen me crying. It turns out, both the pastor and I were unsure of what he preached that night, and I determined from a comment he made from the pulpit during the next service that we had each watched the message the next day on the Internet. God needed to show us certain things respectively.

As I left church, I saw Mama and gave her a huge hug as I passed through the doors. I was then greeted by another woman who asked how I was doing. She gave me a hug and started to speak life into me when I told her that I was in travail. She said, "Birth quadruplets. Get it over in one fell swoop." I laughed, as this was exactly what I needed to hear. Just then, I turned and saw the pastor looking at me and beaming me a big ol' smile, as if he already knew. I gazed back at him. Reviewing the day and all that had taken place, I smiled to myself.

God speaks to me almost daily, and at His direction a year ago, I began to write. I wrote about the words spoken to me and the scriptures I received after praying. Many of the words have come to pass since I started writing, whether they were answered prayers, healings of the heart, breakthroughs, or revelations, all because I was obedient to His voice. And all the instructions, triumphs, and realizations are typed into monthly journals titled *Moving Forward*; I share many of them with candor and transparency in this book.

He can use the Bible, family, friends, complete strangers, a television program, even a bumper sticker to speak directly to each of us. Many people think it is their intuition they are hearing, but the reality is that it is God's soft, still voice they hear. Don't place limits on the ways you hear God speak to you. He can use anything to make a point or answer a question. God is always speaking to us; it's our choice to listen.

CHAPTER 7
Following the Instructions

God asks for obedience, not sacrifice. As it says in 1 Samuel 15:22:

Samuel said, "Has the LORD as much delight in burnt offerings and sacrifices As in obeying the voice of the LORD? Behold, to obey is better than sacrifice, And to heed than the fat of rams.

Over my life as a Christian, I have followed the instructions given to me most of the time. Hearing His voice was crucial to my walk with Him. But it wasn't until I started receiving unlikely instructions that my faith was really tested.

Reflecting back on the prophetic word spoken by the chaplain, it took some time for me to realize that God was instructing me, which I thought would ultimately lead to the fulfillment of the prophecy. Many of the instructions I received over a two-and-a-half-year timeframe resulted in my spiritual growth. Having shared these instructions with a few people, they would acknowledge that I was really trusting God and expressed that they doubted they could ever have followed through with what was asked of me. I realize now that the crazy instructions I obeyed were preparing me for my identity and destiny.

Instruction #1 – During the high holidays of the Jewish calendar, I often attended a Messianic congregation for Rosh Hashanah, Yom Kippur, and the Feast of Tabernacles. At the 2011 Feast of Tabernacles service, the *rebbetzin*[1] announced that the congregation was going to host its first singles dinner on the first Sunday in November. The Lord spoke to me and said, "Attend the singles dinner."

I said, "OK."

The *rebbetzin* spoke again, saying, "Pastor from the church will be the guest speaker, and he will be preaching on the joy of being single."

My spirit flipped like it had never before; it was huge, and I freaked out. The scripture where Elizabeth meets Mary when they were both pregnant came to mind. Luke 1:41 puts it this way:

> When Elizabeth heard Mary's greeting, the baby leaped in her womb; and Elizabeth was filled with the Holy Spirit.

The "flip" was incredible, and I said to the Lord, "I am going to have to pray about attending." I didn't want the pastor to think I was interested or chasing after him. There were enough women in the church who believed God was telling them that the Pastor was to be their husband. I was not one of them.

Think of it, I was telling the Lord I needed to pray about an instruction He gave me. After the service, I went home and began to pray over whether or not to attend the singles dinner. God confirmed my attendance the next day at the Saturday night service. The pastor started talking about the *power of place*. He offered an illustration from his own personal experience about being in a location where God had opened up an opportunity for something in the future. He explained that a place might lead to meeting someone or allowing something to happen by "divine appointment."

On Monday, I contacted the Messianic synagogue to verify whether it would be OK for me to attend the dinner, even though I had not paid on time. I received an email reply telling me to bring my check with me to the dinner. I was obedient to God's first instruction.

I knew the Pastor was going to be there, but he didn't know I would be there until he saw me. Needless to say, he was shocked

---
[1] title used for the wife of a rabbi

and asked someone to find out why I had decided to attend. I simply answered, "It was an instruction from the Lord." What I didn't realize at the time was that this was the first of many instructions the Lord was to give me over the following six-month period.

Instruction #2 – An ice breaker started off the singles dinner, requiring each person to find someone who fell into one of 20 categories listed on a game card. I went to the pastor for the *speaking a second language* category, and later went back to see if he could sign off on any other categories. As he reviewed the categories I still had open, he commented, "I like Mexican food, but I don't love it and I don't have any joy." The irony! For the topic of his message was *The Joy of Being Single*.

    At the end of the evening, each person received a boxed set of thank you cards as a gift for attending. Driving home, the Lord spoke, telling me, "Write the pastor a note." I queried, "About what?"

    The Lord told me, "Write that you are praying for his joy to return." So, I wrote the note, including a few scriptures related to joy, and dropped it into the church mail slot on Monday morning. I also began to pray that his joy would return to him.

    During his message at the Tuesday night service, the pastor mentioned that his joy had returned to him. *Thank you, Jesus, for the answered prayer.* While at the altar praising and praying, I also noticed the power of the Lord present as he walked behind me. I thought to myself, *WOW!*

    Over the next few months I received instructions about what to wear, where to sit, what to say to the pastor, and when to go to the altar. I shared the instructions with a friend from work, who is also a believer. It seemed that every week I received some type of directive. After two or three months of sharing these instructions with my friend, she asked me, "Have you ever thought that the pastor is to be your husband?" At that point, I hadn't. Though I did think it was odd that the instructions always involved him. Then, I began to wonder: *Really? The pastor?*

    When the strong possibility that he was to be my husband finally dawned on me, I remembered my friend saying to me, "Julie, you are so slow!" I honestly think God uses my innocence for just these kinds of things. Shortly thereafter, she said to me, "I have never heard you mention anything about being attracted to him."

I answered her truthfully, "I look at the heart, not the physical appearance." But the Saturday night after she made the comment, I remember God telling me to wear my best suit, and I questioned His direction, as the suit is the nicest ensemble of clothing I own. It was expensive and totally out of character from the clothes I usually wore to the Saturday night service, jeans and a top.

Little did I know what He had planned for me that evening. Sitting off to the side in the second row, I watched the pastor emerge from the side door. When he turned around to talk to someone, I noticed he was dressed in a suit with his shirt open at the collar. His hair had grown out, and for the first time I said to myself, *Now that is how I want my husband to look and dress.* We were both wearing suits at the Saturday night service. I was beginning to think to myself, *Maybe the pastor is my husband.*

The most profound instruction to this point came in February. From the pulpit, the pastor was introducing some single men to the congregation and joked that if any women were interested, they should send their résumés to the church office by 9 a.m. Tuesday. It was all done in jest, but with real meaning behind the words. That's when the Lord spoke again: "Send the pastor your résumé."

I responded, "But he hasn't asked for it."

All of a sudden, someone said from the congregation, "What about you, pastor?"

Sheepishly, he said, "Send your résumé to my attention before 9 a.m. Tuesday." That question and answer were my confirmation.

As I drove home from church on Sunday, God downloaded my entire spiritual résumé. I called my friend in Florida and told her what happened. It took about one-and-a-half hours to draft the resume on paper. I revised it a second time, and on Monday morning, I typed it.

As I wrote and typed, I prayed over the resume. By this point, I was no longer running and believed the pastor was supposed to be my husband. The way I viewed it, God wouldn't have given me such an instruction if that weren't true. I slipped the resume and cover letter into the church mail slot on Monday evening.

With trepidation, I attended the Tuesday service. Having been obedient to the instruction, I was unsure how the résumé might have been received. *It's in God's hands now.* At the end of service, the pastor was waiting for me by the exit. He asked, "Are you the one who…" and with his hands made the shape of the catalog envelope that held my résumé and cover letter. I nodded my head, yes. He proceeded to tell me "no" and thanked me for the prayer.

In the cover letter, I had explained that I was praying Ruth 4:11 for him:

> Then the elders and all those at the gate said, "We are witnesses. May the LORD make the woman who is coming into your home like Rachel and Leah, who together built up the house of Israel. May you have standing in Ephrathah and be famous in Bethlehem. (NIV)

I listened to the pastor, not saying a word. While he continued to reiterate his "no," God showed me a specific sentence in my cover letter that stated "you will be married" and told me to speak. When he finished, I looked at him and said, simply, "You will be." I was referring to the fact that he was going to be married, whether me or someone else.

I was obedient, but unsure of the outcome that had just taken place. At home that night, I prayed and asked God for the purpose of following His instructions. Saturday morning, four days after the pastor said no, I received my answer in the Word, and it was confirmed when I called my friend in Florida. She reminded me of Genesis, Chapter 22, when God tested Abraham and his heart toward God. It was a TEST! So I held onto the belief that Pastor was to be my husband, in spite of the faith test.

Pastor went on vacation following that encounter, and when he returned to the pulpit a week later, he began to preach on Genesis, Chapter 22 and how God tests our heart. At one point in his message, he said, "I didn't realize until this weekend." I was vindicated, but that didn't stop the nasty looks and scrutiny from those in the church who knew what I had done; as I wrote on the résumé that the pastor had permission to share it, if he wished. That scrutiny was the beginning of many dirty looks and avoidance over the next year-and-a-half. I held my head high as I simply did what God had instructed, but that didn't make it any easier when I went to church. I don't know if the pastor thought of me as his wife at that point, but he did know that God was testing me.

Over the next several months, I received instructions to send three specific notes to the pastor. Those instructions and what happened after I sent each note are discussed in Chapter 13, *Exposing Character Flaws*. How we responded and reacted to each other after each note showed me that God needed to do a lot of character development in each of us. I often wondered why God chose me to follow His instructions, instead of the other way around, as it usually involved me doing something that affected the pastor.

When unusual instructions are given, it's tempting to think they aren't from God. Often, He is testing us to see our heart and to learn what we are willing to do for Him. The more outrageous the instruction and the more obedient we are, the more God can trust us with the big things He has planned for each of us. Unsure whether the instruction is from God? Wait for confirmation. I found He always confirmed the instruction when I asked Him to, and it always came from both the Word and the pulpit. I usually waited for at least two confirmations when it came to some of the crazier instructions.

Be encouraged to complete the instruction. In my personal experience, the more outrageous the instruction, the more He used me for His good and glory. And when people doubted that it was God, I was always vindicated. I never asked to be vindicated; God did so because I completed His command.

CHAPTER 8

Confirmations

As the Lord gave me instructions or I questioned something about the pastor being my husband, I always received a confirmation. Sometimes the confirmations came in unusual packages. During the time I was meditating and talking to God about the vision I'd had of the pastor's wife, I received two confirmations on one Sunday afternoon. The first occurred as I watched a well-known bishop on TV and is discussed in detail in Chapter 9, *Prayer for the Pastor's Wife*. The second confirmation occurred when I asked Saki, my son's a sixteen-pound tabby cat, how he would feel about the pastor becoming part of the family.

On Saturday, the pastor shared from the pulpit that he had a desire to get a pet, a small dog, to be exact. I'll never forget him mentioning that everyone he knew was advising him against a pet. He looked at me from the pulpit and asked if he should get a small dog – again, the same question. I shook my head no, as I already had Saki. No need for Pastor to get a pet, when he would automatically inherit one. And Saki is fixed of course, and just the size of a small dog.

By now, I was starting to freak out. A pastor's wife? The reality of the possibility started to cross my mind, but as the confirmations presented themselves, I ran. I ran, knowing the huge responsibility it is to be a pastor's wife. As the former director of a nonprofit women's program, I knew firsthand about being responsible for others, whether it was the staff or the clients we served. I put on my tennis shoes and figuratively started to run. That was December.

Early January, I was led to attend the same Messianic community, on a Friday night. At the end of service, an altar call was given for those who needed *direction*. I went up, and an elder prayed for me. Out of his mouth came the words, "What God has opened, no man can shut," from Revelation 3:8:

> 'I know your deeds. Behold, I have put before you an open door which no one can shut, because you have a little power, and have kept My word, and have not denied My name.

I began to weep. The next day I prayed and opened the Word to Jonah, Chapter 1. It was confirmation that I was running from God and His call to be the pastor's wife. I couldn't believe it – me, a pastor's wife?

It wasn't until February that I accepted the fact the pastor was to be my husband. In fact, I thought giving him my résumé was a confirmation. Now I understand that the résumé incident had been a test from God to see if I would follow His instructions and do His will. Finally accepting the idea, God now had to start working on the pastor.

Case in point. A friend of the pastor's was a guest speaker at church. He gave his testimony about how God was using his cancer as an opportunity to minister to the healthcare professionals who were caring for him. A couple of months passed, and the man was on my heart. The Lord told me, "Ask Pastor how his friend is doing."

I answered, "You need to open up the door for me to say something to him." When I next entered the church, he was standing by himself drinking a cup of coffee. I went up to him and asked how his friend was doing. He told me his friend was doing well and that he had talked with him a few weeks prior.

"Interesting," I told him. "That is exactly how long he has been on my heart." Only God. Peripherally, I saw the pastor watch as I walked to my seat. I know he was amazed, as by this time we were beginning to realize how in tune we were with each other.

One Sunday, the chaplain preached from Genesis, Chapter 22. These were the same scriptures I had received back in February from my friend in Florida, and from the pulpit by the pastor. This time though, the chaplain spoke something the other two had not, Genesis 22:8:

> *Abraham said, "God will provide for Himself the lamb for the burnt offering, my son." So the two of them walked on together.*

The chaplain then said, "Abraham was tested to offer Isaac as a sacrifice, but he trusted God and spoke the *prophetic word* that a sacrifice would be provided by the Lord, which it was."

The comment I had made to the pastor all those months ago was now confirmed by the chaplain. I was vindicated again, this time as it related to marriage and the instructions to speak the short phrase, "You will be." At the end of service, after the last worship song, I opened my eyes and I saw the pastor looking at me. He quickly looked away.

One day, I was joyful and had a song in my heart that I kept repeating. The phrase was "living in the overflow, expect the supernatural," from a song I'd recently heard on the television. As I praised the Lord, I sent a text to all my friends saying, *It is a glorious day in the Lord.*

I received a text back from one friend stating, *I've been praying for you.*

Followed by the same friend texting, *I pray over you God's blessing as He directs your path and gives you the necessary instruction to experience supernatural breakthrough in His perfect will, purpose and plan for your life.* It was confirmation of the song in my heart and what transpired two days later – the thousand-fold increase of faith and a breakthrough to go along with it. That breakthrough was the beginning of other supernatural events that occurred over the next few weeks. This confirmation is discussed in Chapter 19, *Doubt.*

Believing I was going to be a pastor's wife, I needed to learn how to show my future husband my love for him in front of the congregation. God is so faithful, He answered my prayer quickly. The answer came by way of the rabbis who were visiting the church. The *rebbetzin* spoke first and then introduced her husband to the congregation. What she did next was the answer to my prayer. She went over to the rabbi and gave him a huge, warm hug, looking at me as she did it. The rabbi's wife knew she was answering my prayer request. That was Saturday night; it was also the first time I worked in the church bookstore.

Sunday morning was the second day I worked in the bookstore. I knew *rebbetzin* had commented about me to the leadership, by their reaction when they saw me. The woman's ministry pastor came to the bookstore and asked me to look for something in the Lost-and-Found. I replied, "It is only my second day in the bookstore, and I have not seen what you are looking for." I know the *rebbetzin* had mentioned my working in the bookstore on Saturday night. To this day, I don't know what she said, but it was something she saw in or on me. Or perhaps she told them that she answered my question to God, "How do I publically show affection to my husband who is also the Shepherd of the Church?"

Part of God's plan for me, I knew, would be to oversee a women's ministry of some sort, whether within or outside the church. Confirmation that my ministry had begun came on a Saturday, exactly one year after the guest speaker from the California church spoke the word.

Women and an occasional man began coming to me for prayer or counsel. A friend of mine had once told me that God would start with individuals and then bring me before groups as He brought me into the fullness of my ministry. Shortly thereafter, I realized I was ministering to people, which led to me ask the women's ministry pastor if I could share my testimony about praying for a young woman had who committed suicide outside my office window, see Chapter 12, *The Power of Place*. Professionally, public speaking was part of my job and I enjoyed it, but this was the first time I'd spoken to a large audience in a church.

The most prolific confirmation about my husband came on Father's Day. Papa spoke about the vision for the church and looked over at me while speaking on three separate occasions. As he concluded, he affirmed, "By this time next year, Pastor will be joined up on this platform with his beautiful wife." The Holy Spirit descended upon me in that moment.

This was a prophetic word to the pastor and confirmation to me.

A few weeks later, the word and Papa's confirmation were further confirmed by the pastor himself when he preached about the Shunammite woman who told her husband they needed to build an upper room for the man of God, Elisha. As a gift for her taking care of the man of God as he passed by on his journeys, he spoke a word over her, predicting that she would have a son within the year. 2 Kings 4:16-17 states:

> *"About this time next year," Elisha said, "you will hold a son in your arms." "No, my lord," she objected. "Don't mislead your servant, O man of God!"*
>
> *But the woman became pregnant, and the next year about that same time she gave birth to a son, just as Elisha had told her.*
> (NIV)

At the end of the message, the pastor stated, "It's too late; the miracle has begun." With that, we looked at each other.

To further confirm the message, while praying for my miracle (my marriage to pastor) one Monday evening, I opened the Bible by faith and received 2 Kings 4:16-17, the same scripture noted above. This time I was told to bracket verse 17, write *the miracle*, and include the date next to the scripture. I did so.

That next day, the pastor started speaking about birthing the miracle. In disbelief at what was being preached, I opened my Bible to the scripture I had bracketed the day before and showed it to the woman sitting next to me. God was starting to birth something through me, and it was my husband – or at least that is what I thought at the time. Keep in mind, the pastor still had not talked to me and we hadn't even had any contact, except for the occasional handshake. Everything between us was still happening in the glory realm, *as it is in heaven*.

A word of encouragement from the pulpit by a visiting pastor from Greece became a confirmation. He spoke about Elijah, who was told by the Lord that the rain would come. It took seven times of him praying earnestly before the rain cloud came. It was his faith in what the Lord told him that made Elijah continue to pray. The entire story can be found in I Kings, chapters 17 and 18. The Greek pastor looked directly at me while he spoke, encouraging me to have faith and continue to pray for the church pastor as my husband. The next day I thanked him for the encouraging word; he just smiled.

An unusual confirmation came by way of some drawings. After church, a man came up to me at the bookstore and showed me a page with five drawings on it. The first drawing he pointed out was me, then Pastor, then a woman who testified about her newborn son's birth, then another woman I don't remember, and finally his dog. This was the wildest confirmation yet. The drawings of the pastor and me were next to each other. I could understand the drawings of the pastor, the woman giving her testimony, and even his dog, but me? That was a God thing!

Don't limit the ways God decides to confirm His promises. Some of the more unusual confirmations I received came through drawings, songs, and unsuspecting individuals. One such instance happened during a conversation I had with a woman and her husband. The man spoke about coming back to church and how he wasn't going to leave. I said, "It's the first day of the rest of your life."

He commented, "That is exactly what pastor said to me, exactly."

This was a confirmation to him and to me. To him, as he knew he would never forsake God; for me, that through all the waiting and tribulation I endured, the pastor was to be my husband.

When my faith would wane, confirmations always came when I needed them most. God is so faithful; He would continually give me glimmers of hope, just when things looked most hopeless. Even during the *season of waiting,* confirmations came from the pulpit, whether from the pastor himself or a guest speaker. A few instances come to mind.

A pastor of another local church preached one Saturday evening on forgiveness. At the end of the message, he said, "It's not good for man to be alone, especially the preacher man. We are praying you a wife. I have been with Pastor for many years and have had to help him with women who've said, 'God called me to be your wife.' That wasn't God. I have your back, Pastor."

As he made this comment, the Spirit of the Lord came upon me, just like it had done when Papa spoke the word about Pastor's wife a few months back. God never told me I would be Pastor's wife and I never approached him about it. I was given instructions, followed them, and realized I had a choice. God gives us free will. I chose to accept being the pastor's wife, when I said yes to God's instructions and His call for me. Would the pastor say yes to being my husband? I was still waiting for the answer.

Around Valentine's Day, I placed Valentine cards in the offering bucket addressed to the pastor, the music pastor, and Papa and Mama. These were the kinds of cards that kids give each other in elementary school. Each card had the scripture address, 1 Corinthians 13:4-8, written on it. Known as the "love scripture," it says:

> Love is patient, love is kind. It does not envy, it does not boast, it is not proud. It is not rude, it is not self-seeking, it is not easily angered, it keeps no record of wrongs. Love does not delight in evil but rejoices with the truth. It always protects, always trusts, always hopes, always perseveres. Love never fails... (NIV)

On the pastor's card, I also wrote, "The best is yet to come." It was a phrase God gave me when I asked what else I should write on the Valentine card. Fast forward to January of the following year. A guest speaker was preaching, as pastor was using wisdom and taking a break for a week. The guest pastor preached on favor and spoke favor over the church. He then said, "One plus one equals a nation."

I received the statement as, when God joins two people together, a nation is born. Scripture references to this statement can be found in Genesis, chapters 2 through 6, referring to Adam and Eve, and Genesis,

Chapter 17, which tells of Abraham and Sarah, who became the father and mother of the nations. Pastor and I both have a call to the nations, and it will come to pass, but God will direct us on the path He has called us, to reach our respective destinies.

> The Sovereign Lord never does anything without revealing his plan to his servants, the prophets. Amos 3:7 (GNT)

Then, the same visiting pastor walked over to the keyboard and began to sing. It was the first time I had heard it, but the song began with the words "The best is yet to come." I received the song as another confirmation. That was March, and I was still waiting.

As a believer, I struggled with vain imaginations. My thoughts and ideas, not God's. Isaiah 55:8 states:

> "For My thoughts are not your thoughts, Nor are your ways My ways," declares the LORD.

The following circumstances I believe were more confirmations to me, but only the pastor would know if he was actually speaking confirmations to me while I watched the services online during the season of waiting. I believe he was speaking out of the side of his mouth, as God had told me he would do several months earlier.

The first confirmation came when he preached about his personal victory. Although he didn't say what the victory was, he preached from Joshua, Chapter 6. Joshua followed the instructions God gave him, and the walls of Jericho fell. I knew I had followed God's instructions, and now Pastor was preaching about his personal victory and how his walls had come down. I knew he had read the draft book that was put into his hands. At one point in the message, he spoke the following:

> *Trust the Lord. Have faith. God has given His word. And even when it doesn't seem like it is going to happen, until that thing*

manifests, I'm not stopping. I'm not slowing down. I'm going to continue to praise Him. I'm going to continue to trust Him, even when it looks like it's not going to happen. That lets me know that it is going to happen even more. I just said something to somebody. That just lets me know even when it seems that it is getting worse instead of better, that lets me know that something great is about to happen. It's about to manifest itself.

When he said, "This is a word for someone," I knew it was for me. At this time, I was still away from the church and it didn't look like I would be returning, but I continued to trust God for instructions about my eminent return.

During the last week of the year end, another confirmation presented itself. The title of the message was *Put Down the Rock* and was based on Exodus, Chapter 17. During the message, the pastor talked about how God uses others to get us to the place He needs us to be before we can move forward. That sometimes the messenger is not the person or package we want or expect, and it is often the person who loves us the most who is the bearer of the message. He proceeded to talk about when the recipient of the message doesn't want to hear the message. The flesh rises up and we push the messenger away because it doesn't feel good. Pastor had pushed me away with the words he spoke to me during a phone conversation three months prior, although at the time, he didn't know it. Yet again, I was vindicated from the pulpit.

When God heals or disciplines us, it is usually painful, but the pain is for a moment in the bigger picture. Hebrews 12:6 says:

FOR THOSE WHOM THE LORD LOVES HE DISCIPLINES, AND HE SCOURGES EVERY SON WHOM HE RECEIVES."

God was trying to get Pastor to a place of addressing certain issues, and I was the one chosen to be the deliverer of the message. As the message continued, Pastor stated that sometimes the messenger needs to step away. Although the messenger has followed the instructions, the person for whom the message is intended still does not receive it. In such a situation, it was now up to God to deal with the person directly, as there was nothing more the messenger could do for the person, except pray. That is what I did; I prayed fervently for the pastor to arrive at the place God needed him to be, and for the congregation. Many prayers of tears were shed. Proverbs 15:29 says:

> The Lord is far from the wicked, But He hears the prayer of the righteous. (NKJV)

The scripture most often quoted regarding the prayer of the righteous is James 5:16:

> Therefore, confess your sins to one another, and pray for one another so that you may be healed. The effective prayer of a righteous man can accomplish much.

I brought to God's remembrance, "The effective prayer of a righteous man can accomplish much" when I prayed. It is His promise, and I believed it in this circumstance. Toward the end of the message, Pastor said very quietly, "Maybe God will bring the person back to you." He knew who I was to him, yet he pushed me away. But God is faithful, and the mess can become the message. This was my hope for Pastor and myself.

God will always confirm the plan He has for each person. It may be stated in various ways, but the message will ultimately be the same. 2 Corinthians 13:1 says:

> This is the third time I am coming to you. EVERY FACT IS TO BE CONFIRMED BY THE TESTIMONY OF TWO OR THREE WITNESSES.

CHAPTER 9

Prayer for the Pastor's Wife

One of the first things I noticed while attending the church was how many women pined for or thought the pastor was to be their husband. In the Spirit, God would show me women who were falling into a trap of deception. I prayed that the spirit of deception would leave the church and that the scales would be removed from their eyes. In most cases, the woman would eventually leave the church, but I was never sure of the reason.

Within the first two years, I realized through the Spirit of the Lord that the church, although growing, would not reach the heights to which God had called it until the pastor was married. At that point, I began to pray for his wife. I got on my knees and prayed fervently for the woman. The Lord gave me a vision of his wife. She was blond, about twenty-eight years old, and a very righteous woman, so knowledgeable in the Word of God that she had attended either Bible college or had been raised in a Christian home. I wasn't sure, but I knew she was righteous.

At the same time, He gave me Ruth 4:11 to start praying for her and the pastor:

> *All the people who were in the court, and the elders, said, "We are witnesses. May the LORD make the woman who is coming into your home like Rachel and Leah, both of whom built the house of Israel; and may you achieve wealth in Ephrathah and become famous in Bethlehem.*

I started a votive offering to God so that He would bring the pastor's wife to him.

I had no idea at the time, but I was actually praying for myself. The woman in the vision was a mirror image of me. As for the knowledge or righteousness, that is for God and others to decide. I don't consider myself righteous, but God establishes me, so He also knows how others perceive and receive me. During my conversation with Saki and the television program mentioned previously, confirmation presented itself when the bishop said, "How you see yourself and how God sees you are two different things." Oh my goodness! I couldn't believe what I was hearing.

It wasn't until I received an instruction in February during the *season of waiting,* that I fully understood righteousness. God spoke to me early one morning, saying, "Go to the Lutheran church on the corner."

I replied, "But, I will be in Tucson." He then showed me a specific Lutheran Church located at the corner of two major streets in Tucson. I knew where I was supposed to go that upcoming Sunday morning.

When I visited my mom that weekend, she was surprised to hear I was going to a Lutheran Church. It was out of the norm for me, but who am I to put God in a box and think I know best? Having never attended a Lutheran church before, I had no expectations, but I was pretty sure the presence of the Lord would not be there. I was right, but that was OK. He knew that the message to be shared from the pulpit would, when revealed, give me full understanding of my attendance. Only God could do such a thing.

As I waited for the reason, the children received a lesson in front of the congregation. It was profound and an excellent illustration to show both the children and adults what happens when we say things that are either intentional or not. The female priest divided the children into two groups. She showed the kids a tube of toothpaste and asked one group to be the toothpaste squeezers and the other group to put the toothpaste back into the tube after it had been squeezed out. The toothpaste was an analogy for hurtful words and actions. As the kids squeezed the toothpaste, she said, "Sometimes we say and do things that are hurtful to others." She asked the kids who were the toothpaste catchers to try and put the toothpaste back into the tube. Try as they did, the kids were unsuccessful in restoring the toothpaste to the tube.

Then she said, "When we say words or perform actions that are hurtful toward others, it is hard to take them back. We must forgive the person who spoke the hurtful words to us. And we must ask for forgiveness if we were the ones who said the hurtful words." What a powerful illustration and message that we all need to learn.

The service proceeded, and the male priest took the podium to share the main message. It was about how Abraham followed God's instructions and was blessed because he did as instructed; it was a confirmation. The priest spoke from Genesis 12:1-4:

> Now the LORD said to Abram, "Go forth from your country, And from your relatives And from your father's house, To the land which I will show you; And I will make you a great nation, And I will bless you, And make your name great; And so you shall be a blessing; And I will bless those who bless you, And the one who curses you I will curse. And in you all the families of the earth will be blessed." So Abram went forth as the LORD had spoken to him; and Lot went with him. Now Abram was seventy-five years old when he departed from Haran.

He also referenced Romans 4:1-5:

> What then shall we say that Abraham, our forefather according to the flesh, has found? For if Abraham was justified by works, he has something to boast about, but not before God. For what does the Scripture say? "ABRAHAM BELIEVED GOD, AND IT WAS CREDITED TO HIM AS RIGHTEOUSNESS." Now to the one who works, his wage is not credited as a favor, but as what is due. But to the one who does not work, but believes in

> *Him who justifies the ungodly, his faith is credited as righteousness,*

My faith for the pastor as my husband was my righteousness. I had been trusting for a couple years God's spoken word: if I followed the instructions given to me, I would be married. By attending the Lutheran church, I now had the full meaning of righteousness with regards to what I saw in the Spirit about the pastor's wife and her righteousness. I was living in *spiritual reality.* I would never have known to visit the church, but God did! I followed the instructions and I had my answer. Only God.

CHAPTER 10

Waiting

I gave Mama a copy of the prophetic word spoken by the chaplain on a Tuesday night in late May, and we met on the Saturday thereafter, before service. She listened intently as I explained the instructions I had received over the past year-and-a-half. At the end of the conversation, she looked at her watch and said it was time for her pray. The last words I spoke to her were, "God told me the next instruction would come from the pastor."

The following Tuesday, the pastor was not at church, but late Friday afternoon, an email blast went out to everyone on the church's listserve. As a subscriber, I read the email when I checked my account at my mom's house in Tucson at about 5 p.m. I remember reading the email and knew it was meant for me, but I wasn't in Phoenix that weekend. I was devastated.

I noted the title of the illustrated sermon, *The Power and Blessing in Waiting.* When I got up from talking with my mom, I went to her home office, downloaded the service on the computer and watched the live stream. The pastor was finishing up the prelude before the illustrated sermon began. He was dressed so nicely, but I wasn't there. I said to myself, "The Lord knew I wasn't going to be there this weekend." I had to trust God in the whole situation.

I watched the human video. It depicted a man sitting on a park bench with a flower in his hand. Another man walked up to the man with the flower and asked, "What are you doing?"

The man replied, "Waiting."

"Waiting for what?"

"For the woman God has for me."

The conversation continued, and the waiting man mentioned some specific characteristics of the woman he was waiting for. "Needs to be a believer, puts God first over me, has a heart for the ministry, and oh, she's blonde." When I heard blonde, I knew the pastor was expressing his personal desires for a wife through the illustrated sermon. It was yet another confirmation that I was to be his wife.

I was devastated that I wasn't there to encourage him. Perhaps it was a thought of the flesh, but I sensed that he, too, was disappointed I wasn't there to watch the human illustration. There was nothing I could do, as I was in Tucson for the weekend. In the message, he talked about how it is important to wait upon the Lord and let Him do the things He needs to do. I received the word, and ultimately the instruction was, *Wait.* So I continued to do so.

I watched the Sunday service on Monday, and it was even better preaching than the Saturday night service. The pastor added a key point to the message that God had given him early Sunday morning: the waiting was for the benefit of both parties. The process of waiting would eliminate any potential crashes. He used the following illustration of an airplane landing.

Occasionally, airline flights find themselves in a holding pattern in the air, due to unforeseen circumstances on the ground. The passengers are unaware that something is happening on the ground and are anxious to land at their destination, but if the plane lands too soon, a catastrophe could happen. By waiting in the air, the unforeseen circumstances can be eliminated and a safe landing can occur. That was what we were in: a holding pattern.

The following Tuesday, I saw Papa, and he said something to the effect of, "You weren't here this weekend."

"No," I explained. "I was at my mom's in Tucson, but I watched it. I saw it," I said, referring to the human video and message. Papa just gave me a big smile, and I smiled back. I knew that word would get back to the pastor.

Throughout the whole journey, I found it amazing that as much as God was moving in my life and doing things to fulfill His path for me, He didn't seem to be connecting the pastor and me. I kept receiving Proverbs 27:17:

> Iron sharpens iron, So one sharpens another.

The pastor and I were only sharpening each other. I had to believe it was due to the fact that once God put us together, there would be no stopping the ways He would use us for His glory. All the iron burrs would have been removed, so there would be no character adjustments necessary once we were married. These would have taken place in advance of his *finding* me. As Proverbs 18:22 state:

> He who finds a wife finds a good thing And obtains favor from the LORD.

At this point, I continued to wait and trust in God and learn the lessons He had for me during the waiting process. I had to stop analyzing everything and stand on Proverbs 3:5-6:

> Trust in the LORD with all your heart And do not lean on your own understanding. In all your ways acknowledge Him, And He will make your paths straight.

I had to stop asking why something was said or done, to stop trying to figure out the reason behind an action or word. I needed to trust and give the situation to Him; if God decided it was something I needed to know, then He would show me in due season.

I learned a valuable lesson about working and having a husband. Asked to work in the bookstore a few days a month, I thought this might be how the pastor and I would connect. That didn't turn out to be the case, but working in the bookstore showed me that I had put work ahead of my husband toward the end of my marriage. Biblically, the order of things should be: God first, husband second, and family third. God was always first when I was married. Without Jesus, I never would have made it as long as I did in the marriage. As the nuptials began to deteriorate, I continued to focus on my son, but work became more important than my husband. I began to take refuge in my work as a way to escape his nastiness.

As my job responsibilities increased at the agency, so did the problems at home. The more often I had to attend meetings around the state, and especially in Phoenix, the more jealous my husband became. I wasn't spending any more time away from the house – it was the fact that I was not in Tucson. Vain imaginations began to run rampant in his mind. He thought I was having an affair, even though I wasn't. The more jealous and suspicious he became, the angrier he got. This led me to take refuge in my work. The women were most appreciative of the assistance and unconditional love they were receiving from me, and I was receiving love and appreciation in return. We were all in a place where we needed confirmation of who we were: me in Christ and Him loving them through me.

Fast forward eight years. I was working in the church bookstore, and a salvation and restoration call was given. I sensed I was supposed to go up for the restoration call, but I had already committed to working in the bookstore. I was torn about what to do and ended up going to the bookstore instead of the altar. Something began to stir in me; something wasn't right. A day passed before I realized what was bothering me. The Lord showed me that I had chosen work over Him in that moment, just as I had chosen work over my husband during the last few years of our marriage.

I could envision my husband saying to me, "You love your work more than you love me." For the first time, I understood what he had been experiencing and acknowledged that he was right. I chose work over him. At that realization, I ran to my bedroom, got on my knees, and repented. What a lesson. I not only repented and asked God to forgive me, but I asked that I would never have to choose between work and my future husband. I want God first in my life, then my husband, and then our work in ministry.

Another lesson I learned while waiting for my future husband was how to fight on the pastor's behalf. I had already prayed for deliverance from the spirit of anger, but now I was recognizing other areas where I could stand in the gap for him, both for the lifting up and pulling down of strongholds. On a Saturday night in September, I heard, "It broke." I believe the deliverances I was praying for him had come to pass. I also believe the pastor was now able to distinguish between the real and the counterfeit when it came to knowing who was called to be his wife.

Waiting also positioned me to trust God, rather than doubt His promise. This was not an easy accomplishment, as my faith waned every once in a while. Approximately every three months, I questioned whether the promise was ever going to manifest. I was so accustomed to God giving me an instruction and it coming to pass almost immediately that having to wait more than two years for the promise of a husband was a new experience. Instructions to move to San Francisco, move to Hawaii, and stay in Tucson, to name a few, never tested my patience and faith like the instructions related to the promise of a husband. The pastor as my husband was a test of my faith.

When I first realized the pastor was to be my husband. God spoke to me and said, "Wait." After about a year of waiting I gave up on the pastor, deciding the rejection on him was so fierce that he could never really love or be loved and married. It was taking such a long time that I figured the pastor wasn't listening to God's instructions – or he didn't want me as his wife. While talking to the Lord and opening the Word by faith, He gave me the following scripture. Zechariah 10:6 states:

> ... And I will bring them back, Because I have had compassion on them; And they will be as though I had not rejected them, For I am the LORD their God and I will answer them.

I realized that if God wasn't turning His back on the pastor, why should I? It was a faith walk I had never experienced before in my life.

As I continued waiting, God gave me scriptures about the high priests, whose purpose was to minister unto Him. Meditating on the duties of the high priest, I realized during my waiting, that I, too, was to minister unto the Lord, whether it be by reading the Bible, singing praises, or praying. God asks us, as believers, to minister unto Him first, then others, following the first two of the Ten Commandments.

Each of us has the calling of a high priest, and as I waited for the Lord to move me into my ministry, I also waited for direction about serving others. Just as Jesus did nothing without His Father's direction, we also need to wait on the Lord. As John 5:19 states:

> Jesus gave them this answer, "I tell you the truth, the Son can do nothing by himself; he can do only what he sees his Father doing, because whatever the Father does the Son also does. (NIV)

So I continued ministering unto the Lord as I faithfully waited for the pastor to approach me.

Waiting builds character. The longer I waited, the deeper the understanding of the paraphrased scripture – peace that passes all understanding (Philippians 4:7). I don't know if the pastor was waiting for instruction from the Lord, or if the Lord was waiting on the pastor to move from the spiritual into the natural. I simply walked in peace as I continued to wait for the Lord to open the door accordingly.

> Wait for the LORD; Be strong and let your heart take courage; Yes, wait for the LORD. Psalm 27:14

CHAPTER 11
Family and Friends

It was January when I had lunch with a girlfriend and told her about the instructions I had both received and followed. She is a believer and I can discuss spiritual things with her. As I told her everything, I began to weep intensely. I finished by saying, "I think the pastor is my husband." This was the first time I had ever professed the statement out loud to anyone. My weeping became uncontrollable, confirming what I spoke. When I speak something and begin to cry, I know I am speaking the truth, whether the word is for me or someone else.

It took a while before I realized that Mama was coming up to me at every service and shaking my hand. It was springtime, and she must have been doing it for three or four weeks before I thought to myself, "Mama is shaking my hand a lot." At first, I was unsure of what to do, so I decided to take it to the Lord in prayer. Around the same time, I realized she was shaking my hand, the rabbis were guest speakers at the church on a Saturday night. The *rebbetzin* shared how God had moved them to the islands, as the result of a word spoken over them at least two years prior to their move.

At the end of the message, she asked if anyone in the congregation had received a vision or dream which still had yet to come to pass. She invited those who answered affirmatively to come to the altar. I went up so quickly and planted myself front and center, as I knew the promise God had given me without a shadow of a doubt. As I stood at the altar, I noticed the pastor praying, with his hand extended in my direction. The rabbi came by and placed his hand on my head and prayed in his heavenly language. I knew God was moving.

Between Mama shaking my hand and the rabbis praying for dreams that hadn't yet come to pass, something began to stir in my spirit. Then the pastor preached a message titled *Issues, Instructions, Incredible Miracle* the following day in May. It was another word that added to the stirring. The stirring was so intense that I needed to talk to Mama as soon as possible. It couldn't wait until the Tuesday night service, so I called her at home on Monday. Papa answered and said she was unavailable, so I left a message. She returned my call about two hours later.

We spoke for about thirty minutes, and I asked if I could take her to lunch or dinner, as I needed to talk in person. It was urgent that I share how God was moving in my life with regards to her son and all that had transpired over the past one-and-a-half years. I believed now was the time, but I really didn't understand what I was doing, except trusting God. She said we needed to pray and then talk after.

I agreed, and at the end of the conversation, she told me she loved me. I was in shock and I said, "I love you too, and Papa, and even Pastor." After the conversation and comment stating she loved me, I was good and didn't feel the need to share any further. However, I took the prophetic word with me to the Tuesday night service, in case she wanted to talk. During praise and worship, she looked at me with a questioning face that said, "Where were you? I thought we were going to talk." In that moment I needed to give her the prophetic word spoken by the chaplain.

After the service, I went to her, handed her the paper with the word typed out, and suggested that we talk on Saturday. I also told her that she was my spiritual mother, which she smiled and received. We talked on Saturday before the service. The following Saturday, the pastor presented and preached the illustrated sermon, *The Blessing and Power in Waiting*. I knew he had talked with his mother.

It didn't matter what I shared with others about what God was doing in my life with regard to the pastor – almost no one supported or believed it. It took two years and many negative comments before I realized that this was my faith walk. My friends who were *believers* in Jesus neither had the faith nor could even believe what I was telling them.

God encouraged me, in spite of all the negative comments, when I opened the Word by faith and received Isaiah 37:6:

> Isaiah said to them, Thus you shall say to your master, 'Thus says the LORD, Do not be afraid because of the words that you have heard, with which the servants of the king of Assyria have blasphemed Me.

To me, this scripture means not to worry about what others say. "Keep your eyes focused on Me, for I am the One who establishes you, not they." I have remembered, "Do not be afraid of the words that you have heard" on many occasions. Ultimately, my friends didn't believe me, or what God was doing between the pastor and me, as everything was taking place in the spiritual.

Strangely, my friends who are not believers received what I was telling them more easily than those who do believe in Jesus. I remember a message the pastor preached a few years ago about Paul shaking off the viper. Acts 28:3-5 states:

> Paul gathered a pile of brushwood and, as he put it on the fire, a viper, driven out by the heat, fastened itself on his hand. When the islanders saw the snake hanging from his hand, they said to each other, "This man must be a murderer; for though he escaped from the sea, Justice has not allowed him to live." But Paul shook the snake off into the fire and suffered no ill effects. (NIV)

Like Paul, sometimes we just need to shake off the negative comments.

The only people who knew and supported me throughout this time were Mama and Papa, and because of all the attacks on the prospective marriage, even they waivered. But God is faithful and He took us all to new heights in faith and purification.

During many conversations with my friend in Florida, with whom I continually shared all the details of what was happening between the pastor and me, one day she said, "Well, I must be looking at this from a worldly perspective." That was it! I received such revelation. She was right. The pastor hadn't asked me on a date, but it was as though we were dating spiritually. We were getting to know one another in the Spirit, or Heaven, before He brought the relationship to fruition on earth. With this revelation, I looked at what was happening between us differently. I had a new perspective, which made me less anxious and explained why the pastor was not inviting me for coffee, lunch or dinner – a date. Church was the common ground where we learned about each other spiritually. I waited for the spiritual to manifest in the natural, as I needed to know Pastor, the man.

Eventually I stopped telling people what was happening, as they couldn't receive it. The good, the bad, and the ugly – I experienced it all. I was thankful for how all the events took place: the character adjustments, the dross, the joys, and the pain before the courtship would be manifested in the natural.

Instructed to keep a journal in July, a month later God directed me to start writing a book about all that was happening between the pastor and me. As I wrote one night, Mac's then-girlfriend asked me what I was typing. I had about sixteen typewritten pages drafted at that point, and I explained that the book was the testimony of God joining my future husband and me. She wanted to know the name of my husband. Hesitant at first to share, I finally mentioned the pastor's name, and she replied, "Oh, Mac already told me that."

Turning to Mac, I asked him how he knew, and he responded that he had known for about a year. Go figure. I proceeded to tell the two of them a few of the many things God had done in my life over the past two years. Mac's girlfriend couldn't believe what she was hearing. Mac just listened and didn't comment, except to say that the pastor's name was on my white board at work, so he figured it out. I explained that his name was on the board because he is the pastor of the church and as such, he needs prayer continually. I know God spoke to my son about my future husband, as he hears God's voice.

Time progressed, and the pastor was not getting any closer to bringing the spiritual into the natural, so my friends began to question the character of the pastor. They questioned his comments to me, his lack of discernment, etc. I explained to all of them that we all sin and fall short of the glory of God. We cannot judge what God was doing in his life and why he reacted to the situations as he did. I had to trust God and follow the instructions given to me, whether my friends supported me or not. Many did not support me, but that was OK; it was my faith walk and test, not theirs. The outcome of the walk was up to the pastor. He could do God's will or his own free will. We have free will to choose Jesus as our Lord and Savior; the pastor could choose me as his wife or not.

CHAPTER 12

The Power of Place

The saying, "in the right place at the right time for the right reason" is often spoken by pastors. The *power of place* can have a lifelong effect on our lives and destinies. Whether it is being obedient to God's call when He sends us somewhere or being in the usual place when God sends someone to us, a divine appointment may be waiting or ready to happen. The first time I experienced the power of place as it pertained to the pastor was detailed in Chapter 7, *Following the Instructions.* It's interesting that that Sunday dinner was the one and only time the singles from the Messianic synagogue ever met. It was as if the whole night, the ice breaker and the dinner, were orchestrated by God for the pastor and me, though neither of us had any idea at the time.

Often, the Lord would instruct me to sit in a specific place in church. One such time was the evening I sat in the back of the church. The usual spots where I sat were all taken, so I ended up sitting in a different place. I was out of my comfort zone, but as the praise and worship took place, God spoke to me and said, "I have positioned you here for a specific reason." At that point, I had no idea what the reason might be, but as the praise and worship continued, God started to use me as a vessel to usher in His presence. Since I was seated at the back, the pastor and Papa could see how God used me as I extended my arm and the Glory of the Lord fell upon the church.

It was the first time they had actually seen God use me as an instrument. That Saturday was outreach, and both Papa and Mama were there, which was out of the ordinary. I remember someone commenting on their presence at the outreach and wondering why they were in attendance. I believed I knew why, but I simply said, "I don't know." Maybe this was the first time the pastor's parents realized that I was his wife, or at least they saw something in me.

During a time of intense scrutiny at work, a young female committed suicide by jumping off the building where I worked. The chain of events is as follows:

It was about 4:15 p.m. on a Tuesday afternoon. A man was talking loudly to anyone who would listen, saying that someone had committed suicide by jumping. After about five minutes of hearing him talk, my supervisor walked over to the window where the man was standing and I followed. As I looked out from the second floor, I saw a paramedic covering up a body with a white sheet.

I said immediately, "I have to pray," and began to pray, "Heavenly Father in the name of Jesus..." The man looked at me and left via the elevator. Less than a minute later, my supervisor also left the hallway. Now alone, I stretched out my hand, as if over the body, and continued, "I pray for this person's salvation, that they know You as their Lord and Savior..." I didn't know what else to pray, so I began to pray in my heavenly language. As I prayed, a peace overwhelmed me. After finishing my prayer, I returned to my office, which was about thirty feet from the window.

I sat down, and the Holy Spirit quickened me to return and pray again. I walked back to the window and stretched out my hand a second time. This time, I prayed for the person's family. Again, I had a peace that passed all understanding. I knew everything was good, and as far as I was concerned, the person had gone to be with the Lord. I learned before I left work that the young woman who had jumped to her death was a senior at the university.

A few days later, the woman who served as the liaison between the deceased young woman's family and the university advised that condolence cards could be dropped off in the department where she worked. I wrote a card and told the family that when I had prayed over their relative, I had peace and believed she had gone to be with the Lord, among other things I don't remember.

A few months after this episode, the liaison came to my office and asked if I was the Julie who had prayed over the young woman. I told her I was, and the woman explained that the mother of the student wanted to contact me. She told me she would give the mother my address at the university.

It amazes me how God orchestrates everything. A few more months passed, and the mom was on my heart. I'd never heard from her, which I thought was strange, especially since she made an effort to confirm who I was. But in August, God brought the mom and me together. It came about in this manner.

A student worker in our department walked into my office early one morning, along with another young woman. We were introduced, and the young woman proceeded to tell me that she had been friends with the student who committed suicide and had seen and talked with the girl's mother the night before. During their conversation, the mom mentioned that she was trying to get a hold of "Julie," but wasn't having any success. The mother mentioned the department I worked in, and the friend instantly interrupted their conversation to send a text.

It happened that the friend had classes with our department's student worker and knew how to contact her, which is how the two young ladies came to show up in my office. After about fifteen minutes of talking, I gave the family friend my business card with my personal contact information on it. That was a Wednesday. Thursday afternoon, my cell phone rang. It was the mother of the young woman I had prayed over. We talked for about a half-hour. She shared personal anecdotes about her daughter, and I told her explicit details of my actions the day her daughter died. We both cried throughout the conversation. At one point, she said to me, "You were the chosen one." I didn't consider myself chosen, as I would have done the same for anyone. This was not the first time I had been witness to a dead body. I am usually led to stop and pray for the person, as was the case for the student.

The mom was so blessed to know someone had prayed over her daughter that she suggested we meet. I asked, "Would you honor me by coming to the church I attend?" I gave her the details of service dates and times, and she agreed to meet me for the Saturday 7 p.m. service. The mother, aunt, and sister of the young woman came to church, and when I met them, they greeted me with two dozen beautiful pink roses. I lost it.

I cried on-and-off for the twenty minutes we talked. They left before service started, as I believe they may have been uncomfortable. The mom told me that she and her daughter were Mormon, and the aunt was Catholic. What is so precious about the church is its diversity. Business people sit next to people who have just come in from the street, and no judgment is passed on anyone. The congregation is culturally diverse, as well, and when a young family who was not polished sat behind us, I could see the discomfort rise up in the three women. They said they had to be somewhere else at 7:30 p.m. I understood and walked them out to their car.

I now had faces to match the names and a family to associate with the young woman I had prayed over. I was emotionally distraught and continued to cry throughout the entire service. During this service, the pastor preached "Blessed are you who are cursed for My name's sake," *The Blessing of the Enemy.* Six days earlier, the pastor had told me not to shake his hand or give him any more notes. I believe he thought the reason I was crying was because of his words and actions toward me. That had nothing to do with it.

When the suicide happened, I knew I was in the precise place I was supposed to be. It was the power of place. As I shared my testimony about this episode at the women's ministry meeting six months later, I knew that even though I had been under extreme duress during this time at work, it was worth it. *I was in the right place for the right time, for the right reason.* If praying for the student was the reason I was in the department, it was worth all the discomfort I had been experiencing for all those months.

While I was in between ministries from the church, the *places* God used me were now outside of the congregation. In fact, from the pulpit the pastor spoke about moving onto other people when the person God puts in your path to help isn't receiving the message. "Step away and move onto someone who will receive the message," he suggested. It turns out, God would put people in my path to minister to, and they were usually people on the Metro Light Rail. People who ride the train can generally be categorized as commuters, of which I am one, students, the less fortunate, and the occasional tourist. I was used by God on many occasions, but three instances were special to me.

The first special encounter happened on my way home from work one day. A man in a wheelchair boarded the train. He sat across from me, and I began to pray for him. He was disabled and drinking from a can wrapped in a paper bag. It smelled like beer. As I prayed, he spilled the beer on himself. I took some facial tissue out of my purse and handed it to him. He wiped himself off and began to talk to me. He had to repeat himself a few times before I understood him, as he told me that he'd had a stroke and life since the stroke had been become difficult. As we continued to talk, he began to cry. My stop was approaching, so when I stood to exit, I whispered in his ear, "God has you in the palm of His hand."

He looked up at me and said, "Put your hand in the hand of the Man who stills the waters." I smiled. Then it dawned on me: that was a song I used to know in the 70s! I began to sing: "Put your hand in the hand of the Man who stills the waters. Put your hand in the hand of the Man who calms the sea. Take a look at yourself, and you can look at others differently, by putting your hand in the hand of the Man from Galilee."

"Oh my gosh!" I thought to myself. "That song is about Jesus." I had heard the song many times growing up, yet I had no idea. Written by Gene MacLellan in 1971, the song was originally sung by Anne Murray and then covered by a Canadian band named Ocean. It now has a new and special meaning to me.

The next two divine appointments led to God fulfilling a desire of my heart after being obedient to His direction. The first appointment happened on a Monday morning while on the train going to work. A homeless couple stepped onto the train yelling at each other. The woman was crying and sat in a different section from the man. I began to pray for them. As I prayed, the man said to the woman, "I don't want to fight, and I'm getting off at the next stop."

The woman, who was still crying, said, "Go ahead." A few stops passed, and the man got off the train, but he re-entered the train through a door behind the woman's seat. Led to talk to the woman, I got up, went over, and sat down next to her.

I said, "That man loves you, but he doesn't know how to show it. He has a spirit of rejection on him. I know, as I was married to rejection for twelve years." I began to cry with her.

She shared some intimate details about herself and her husband with me, and I asked if I could pray for her. She agreed. Holding her hand, I began to pray. At the end of the prayer, she said, "Thank you for letting me know he loves me."

Toward the end of the conversation, God had already told me to give her the money in my wallet. She told me she was hungry and really wanted a warm breakfast. I gave her all the money in my wallet, except for the six dollars I would need to buy a ticket to a Christmas pageant I'd planned to attend that night. I also gave her my business card and the church's card and told her that if she was serious about getting off the street, the church could help her. She exited the train, thanking me profusely. In turn, I thanked God for using me as an instrument of His love.

The next ordained encounter happened Friday of the same week. A woman boarded the train and sat across from me. She was obviously homeless, as she had many bags settled next to her. God spoke, and said, "Despondent." Then He said, "Give her five dollars." I had asked my son for change for a twenty the previous night, and he'd given me two fives and a ten, so I had the correct amount in my wallet. For some reason, I knew I needed to act quickly, like I could lose out on the blessing of helping her out. I took the money out of my wallet, got up, walked over to her, and said, "I'm supposed to give this to you."

She looked at the money, then at me, and said, "Thank you." She closed her eyes, and tears began to roll down her face. Then my eyes welled up with tears. She got off at the next stop, mouthing "God bless you" as she exited. Yet she doesn't have any idea how much I was blessed by our interaction.

The following week, God fulfilled a desire of my heart. Although I have been healed of the pain related to it, I am still somewhat self-conscience of my skin and take care of it to this day. If I can afford it, I treat myself to a facial every eight weeks. One of my desires was to have a collagen boosting treatment to reduce the size of my facial pores, but the procedure is expensive. However, God knows my desires and how to fulfill them. I received an email from the med spa I use for some of my personal care services offering a free collagen treatment. I signed up immediately! I knew that because I had been obedient to the assignments He had presented, God was now fulfilling the desire of my heart. As Psalms 37:4-5 says:

> Delight yourself in the LORD; And He will give you the desires of your heart. Commit your way to the LORD, Trust also in Him, and He will do it.

The med spa is a *place* that I have been going to for a few years. The electrologist is fascinated to hear the stories I tell her about the things God has done in my life since my previous visit. In fact, she is usually the one who asks about the pastor or the monthly outreach. Many times, when I have shared something with her, she has gotten goose bumps, which is always a confirmation to me.

The most telling goose bump inducing story was about the time I was *in between ministries*. I shared with her that after a month of not attending church had passed, only one person had contacted me to find out if I was OK. I mentioned that I thought it didn't say much for the congregation; she got goose bumps. But I continued, explaining that it was OK that no one contacted me, as I didn't particularly want to explain the situation anyway. I was better left alone, than have to explain the pastor's words to me. I believe that sharing my personal experiences and relationship with Jesus are watering the seed planted in her.

The next significant place God directed me to go opened unexpected doors to my destiny. It started with an invitation from the California pastor to attend a women's ministry meeting at another church. As I waited for direction, I entered a place of rest, which is a wonderful place to be!

CHAPTER 13

Exposing Character Flaws

Over a seven-month timeframe, I was instructed to write and give three notes to the pastor on three separate occasions. I sent the first note in February, the second in July, and the final note in August. Each note related to a specific instance, and the response to each exposed character flaws in both the pastor and myself. God used the notes for His glory as He worked to transform our characters and bring us to the place we needed to be in order to be husband and wife, serve in the ministry together, and accomplish the things He had called us to do.

The first note, I thought, was an instruction; after prayer, however, I decided it was my vain imagination. Either way, the note caused havoc for me, just like the résumé instruction. What a learning experience; it brought hidden things to light for Pastor and myself. The chain of events occurred as follows:

Over a period of time, I sensed that Pastor wanted me to do something, but I didn't know what it was. Well before God told me the pastor would be speaking words out of the side of his mouth, he would speak words from the pulpit and I didn't know if they were for me, so I wrote a note to the pastor where I mentioned that unless he pointed in my direction or I truly knew he was looking at and talking to me, I was unsure of the intent of the message he was trying to get across. I included my phone number in the note, telling him that if I was failing to understand something he wanted me know on a spiritual level, he should call me. In the note, I also wrote, at the Lord's prompting, *Are you ready to cross the Jordan?*

Well, he called immediately upon reading the note and proceeded to ask the same question again and again, something that I don't even remember now, without allowing me to respond. I thought to myself and the Lord, "Whatever I say, he is not going to hear it." I tried to explain at one point, but he kept talking over me. Finally, at the end of the one-sided conversation, he asked, "What's the meaning of, *Are you ready to cross the Jordan?*"

I answered simply, "I don't know," because I didn't want to impose my thoughts about how God intended him to receive the message. When I wrote it, it meant to me, was he ready to cross the Jordan with me, to begin our life and ministry together?

Then he asked, "Why did you write the note?"

I responded, "I didn't want to." But it's not that I didn't want to write it; I had been in prayer about sending the note for a few weeks. On the train into work one morning, I came to the conclusion that the idea to send the note was my vain imagination, and at that point, I had a peace. But as I was working, I heard, "Send the note," and as far as I believed, it was the Lord speaking to me.

I had brought a notecard to work, just in case I should be prompted to write the note. Since the idea had been stirring in my spirit for a while, I decided that once I had a peace about writing it, I would. I wrote the note on a Monday morning and dropped it off at church that night. Pastor called midday on Tuesday. The unfortunate thing is what should have come out of my mouth was, "I didn't want to, because I thought it was my vain imagination to send the card." That would have explained everything, but instead, I said, "I didn't want to," and the conversation spiraled downward thereafter.

I believe the pastor now interpreted my lack of words as saying I didn't want to send the card at all. As if I was being disobedient to God and I didn't really care about Pastor or encourage him. That was the farthest thing from the truth; I did care about him and I wanted to encourage him. The devil is a liar and, boy, did the enemy have a heyday with my sharp tongue. Those words hurt the pastor, when the note should have been an encouragement to him.

He made a comment about everything being "all good" and I answered, "Yes." He commented about the possibility of me moving to another church, and I responded, "Why would I do that? God called me to this church." What transpired after that conversation changed both of us and our growth in the Lord. The spirits of a sharp tongue in me and anger in him had now surfaced for the first time, and the ways we allowed God to take us through our respective processes would determine our destinies.

To this day, I do not know if it was my vain imagination or an instruction from God. Although I have asked for the answer, I have yet to know if it was Him, my flesh, or the enemy I heard regarding that note. I now found myself standing on the promise in Romans 8:28:

And we know that God causes all things to work together for good to those who love God, to those who are called according to His purpose.

When anger manifested in the pastor, I told the Lord, "I can't live with that. I was married to anger for twelve years, but I will pray for him." At that moment, I decided to pray for him and his deliverance, rather than say "no" to being his wife. I prayed for about three weeks or so, asking God to deliver him of anger. This was now a test of my faith!

At the same time I started to pray against anger, I was asked to care for the children of the adults who went out on the church's monthly outreach. To help instill biblical teaching into the kids, I shared the story of Joshua: by his walking around the walls of Jericho seven times, the strongholds were pulled down and the Israelites had the victory. The complete story is found in Joshua, Chapter 6. I asked each child what they wanted to pray about, and interestingly many of the kids said they didn't want their parents to fight anymore – anger, again. So we diligently prayed and walked around the church parking lot seven times, pulling down the stronghold of anger, along with other bondages. It was a symbolic gesture that I continue to perform to this day.

Five to six weeks later, Papa, who is Pastor's dad and the church prophet, started praying in his heavenly language; then he gave the interpretation. His word was, "The spirit of anger no longer exists."

I yelled, "YES, YES, YES!" I knew it was an answer to the prayer the kids and I had prayed weeks earlier. God is so faithful.

Around the same time, God began teaching me about scrutiny. Because of the note, all of a sudden, the church leadership began questioning me and my actions. Not only was I experiencing scrutiny from the church, but I was also dealing with intense scrutiny in my workplace. The pressure was intense in both places, but I continued to trust the Lord and His promises. And this wasn't a week or two of scrutiny – it went on for more than a year.

A few months went by and Romans 8:28 came to pass.

What the enemy meant for evil now just took pastor and me to another level in the Lord. It worked out for God's glory: Pastor, I presumed, was delivered from anger, and I persevered through the storm of hurting him with my words. God started to move in us again. The pastor and I received confirmation by someone giving their testimony. The person stated that even in difficult times in relationships, if God has His hand on the relationship, no one can shut the door. We just looked at each other.

The second note was definitely of the Lord. After about three weeks of waiting, the confirmation came; when it did, I sent the note. I sent it after receiving a phone call from the pastor one night. It was a Wednesday evening when my cell phone rang. The caller ID came up *Unknown*. I said hello twice, but the caller hung up. The only other time *Unknown* had come up on my caller ID in the ten years I have had this phone number was when pastor called me after reading the first note. I don't know why he called, and I wasn't going to let vain imaginations start working in my mind again. I let it go.

When I received confirmation from the pulpit, I sent a note that read, "Be encouraged. Next time don't hang up. I look forward to talking with you." I mailed the note on Monday, and he received it the next day. This note was better received by Pastor than the first one, but it could have been better still. This note generated resistance on both of our parts. With Papa as a witness, Pastor kept asking me the same question: "What do you want to talk about?"

Again, my answer was, "I don't know." That is the only thing that would come out of my mouth, even though I had many ideas for things to discuss in my head.

Pastor closed the conversation the same way he did the first conversation, with "We're good?" Yes, I was good, and as far as I was concerned, things were still fine. I knew who he was to me; it was just another instance where God was working in us. The good thing was my sharp tongue failed to surface this time, and pastor wasn't angry. I was prompted to smile at him during the whole service that evening, and the pastor watched me, not knowing why. But I knew God was still dealing with us about something. The pastor was now creating his own rejection, and although I didn't know it at the time, I still didn't know how to respond or talk to the man.

From the pulpit, Papa this time gave me a word of encouragement, Isaiah 59:1:

*Behold, the LORD's hand is not so short That it cannot save;
Nor is His ear so dull That it cannot hear.*

I was sitting on the aisle and as he passed by my chair, and we sideglanced at each other. We both knew God can do anything, and He was doing it. Over the next few services, Pastor preached how resistance propels us forward, and we need to listen if something is happening a second time. It was great teaching. He used Paul's voyage to Rome in Acts 27 to convey this, explaining how Paul told the people on the boat to do one thing, but they ignored him. This led to problems, but eventually they listened when he made the suggestion a second time. God was using me and the second note to propel the pastor to another level and to deliver him from rejection. At the time, I didn't think the situation had anything to do with me. It was more than a year later, while attending another church, that I received the full understanding of my own insecurities in talking to men.

The third note came about after seeking an answer as to why the pastor had stopped shaking my hand. The scripture below was the answer to my question, which led me to write the third and final note. This note reflected nothing but love and prophetic words, addressing handshakes, among other things. In the note, I wrote that I was unsure whether it was an instruction from God to the pastor, but I had noticed a difference in his handshake when he shook my hand when leaving the church; it was now limp and lifeless. 2 Kings 10:15 was my confirmation that something was different:

> Now when he had departed from there, he met Jehonadab, the son of Rechab, coming to meet him; and he greeted him and said to him, "Is your heart right, as my heart is with your heart?" And Jehonadab answered, "It is." Jehu said, "If it is, give me your hand." And he gave him his hand, and he took him up to him into the chariot.

I wrote the note on white paper, placed it inside a thank you card, and gave it to him while his parents were on vacation. He would have to deal with this note by himself. I knew the exact time he was reading it, as an anointing came over me while I worked in the bookstore on a Sunday. The woman who was working with me experienced it as well. I just starting praising and thanking the Lord. Next thing I knew, Pastor was heading toward me. I moved to meet him by the counter opening.

He was so angry, telling me, "No more handshakes and no more notes." Then he commented that it was only God's grace that kept me working in the bookstore and the next time it happened, I would be kicked out of the church.

He handed the note back to me, and I graciously accepted it, saying, "OK, OK." The service began, and two young men were sharing from the pulpit and teaching, instead of the pastor. Both preached on *Moving Forward*. The words were very appropriate, and shortly into the first message, I heard "convicted," and the Lord gave me Judges 4:14:

> Deborah said to Barak, "Arise! For this is the day in which the LORD has given Sisera into your hands; behold, the LORD has gone out before you." ...

I knew God had this one again!

On Tuesday, Pastor was fairly quiet as the Lord moved in the service. My guess is that God was dealing with him about how he had reacted toward me and the note. I went to the altar for praise and worship, and at the end, I looked up and saw the music pastor beaming a big ol' smile at me. He knew I was standing in the gap, praying for Pastor. I prayed against those spirits I believed were holding him back from going to the next level. Walls were going to be pulled down in the Pastor, and I was the one to pray for it to happen. Who better to pull down the strongholds than I, his future wife?

I knew the day would come when he would again shake my hand, and the circumstance under which the handshake would occur would be ordained by God. It was eight or nine months from the time he originally told me to stop shaking his hand before he extended his hand to me again.

Saturday's service came, and it was his best preaching ever! Unfortunately, that service was the same night the mother of the young woman who had committed suicide came to church. Talking to her wrecked me, and I was a crying mess. I received the word that he was preaching, but it wasn't until the Tuesday service that I was able to rejoice about the message. He preached from Matthew 5:11-12:

> "Blessed are you when people insult you, persecute you and falsely say all kinds of evil against you because of me. Rejoice and be glad, because great is your reward in heaven, for in the

same way they persecuted the prophets who were before you. (NIV)

What's interesting about the message is that I never thought of Pastor's reaction as persecution, as I knew he was involved in a spiritual battle. God was still working in him, trying to get him somewhere. I watched the original message from Saturday and noticed he was directing a lot of his preaching toward where I sat. The word he spoke during the message was profound, yet I don't remember hearing it, due to the duress I was experiencing over the mother's grief. He said, "I'm coming, I'm coming. I'm getting there; no, I am there." I knew he was referring to what God was doing in him, and that he would get to where God wanted him to be so that He could put us together.

Character flaws were exposed, and there was work to be accomplished in both of us. Willing to stay in the process, only time would bring me to the place God had ordained. Not knowing what He was accomplishing in the pastor, based on his preaching and teachings over the next several months, God was dealing with him, as well.

When God brings to light those characteristics that He wants to deliver us from, how we accept the correction and lesson and move forward will determine our destiny. I thought it was all about the pastor, but it was about me too, although I did not recognize this at the time. Time can be our friend: be open for the lesson to reveal itself when you are ready to receive it.

CHAPTER 14
Hinderances and Deliverances

Romans 3:23 says:

for all have sinned and fall short of the glory of God,

Sin can be a hindrance to the destiny God has for each of us, and the pastor and I had our share of hindrances from which we needed deliverance. This topic, is addressed not to judge, but to explain God's grace and mercy.

One of the very first scriptures God instilled in me when I was first born again was Matthew 7:5:

"You hypocrite, first take the log out of your own eye, and then you will see clearly to take the speck out of your brother's eye.

I still live by this word and try not to judge others. Where a person is in their walk with the Heavenly Father, how they dress, act, or speak is not for me to say.

So I start by taking the log out of my own eye, before taking the speck out of anyone else's. Probably the biggest obstacle in my Christian walk was the spirit of criticism that was passed to me as a generational curse from my father's side of the family. The spirit didn't manifest itself as criticism in me, but what I refer to as a *sharp tongue*. Words came out of my mouth that I didn't mean to say. It was as if they would get twisted or I would speak an incomplete sentence, so the words would be taken out of context or the intent of what I really meant. Having asked the Lord to remove the nasty spirit for years, my tongue was sharp, but not as sharp as it used to be. My words could be damaging, but most of the time, the Lord would quicken me, and I would ask the person to forgive me. This is a very humbling experience at any time.

Following the conversation resulting from the first note, the pastor was so angry with me. From the congregation, I said, "I'm sorry. I'm sorry." He saw me, as did the music pastor. Actually, the music pastor was out of place, as if God had moved him so he could see me apologize to the pastor. The music pastor was my witness as I apologized to the senior pastor. The pastor spun around, placing his back to me. Seeing her son turn around quickly, Mama looked around in an effort to determine who her son was looking at. She saw me.

Fast forward six months to the time I was invited to a healing clinic by a woman from church. I knew I was to attend, but I didn't know why. Out of obedience I went, and God delivered me from a sharp tongue in that moment. It was an answer to a prayer I had prayed for countless years. A woman who has a deliverance and healing ministry was teaching, and she told everyone to start asking for their healing, though not necessarily a physical healing. She said to bind the strongman, so it didn't come back. I asked God to heal and deliver me from my sharp tongue.

As I prayed, the woman asked, "Julie, are you here?" I raised my hand. It turned out I was the only Julie in the audience. She started to speak, "There is something about your father." I nodded my head yes. "I see a donut. About five years ago." Then she repeated, "There is something about your dad."

I said, "A spirit of criticism, a generational curse."

She spoke, "God has healed you now."

It took a couple of days to digest what happened, as it was serendipitous that I was praying for deliverance from criticism as she was calling my name. I wondered if it was a familiar spirit she was tapping into. And what did the part about the donut mean? A few days later, I recalled the comment and the situation. One weekend, about five years prior, I'd been visiting my parents. I was eating a donut when my dad told me I would get fat if I continued to eat donuts.

I meditated on whether the statement was from a false prophet; I needed to be sure it was God. Helping clean the church the following Tuesday, I asked a woman who was cleaning with me, and who had also attended the healing clinic, what exactly the woman said to me about being delivered; she told me. Instantly, I knew it was God, and I was delivered. To my knowledge, I have not spoken words with a sharp tongue since that Friday evening. Thank goodness for obedience.

The enemy tried using the words the pastor and I spoke against each other throughout the whole *spiritual dating* process. Never have I experienced such spiritual warfare in my life. Now I was delivered; no more sharp tongue, and as time passed, I became passive to the words and anger proceeding from the pastor's mouth. The enemy no longer had a hold on me.

Low self-esteem was the other demon I struggled with all my life. This had to do with the criticism I received from my dad, which was almost always about my appearance. I can now say that I was blessed with bad skin, but in my teens and early twenties, I had very oily skin, which created many skin problems that resulted in large pores and breakouts that persist to this day. The blessing behind the bad skin is that I look much younger than my chronological age.

That being said, my parents didn't consider taking me to a dermatologist or buying me skin care products that might have reduced or prevented the breakouts. This episode from my early years is still difficult to share because of all the pain I endured at the voice and hand of my dad. The voice related to his comments about my bad skin, poor posture, or weight and his hand because he wanted to pick at my face. I was always thin; even my paternal grandma, from whom the generational curse originates, told me I was too skinny and needed to eat more food. At one point, she even offered me a dollar a pound if I gained weight; but that never happened, as my metabolism was high and it didn't matter how much or how little I ate.

The Word tells us we are created in His image. Genesis 1:27 says:

> God created man in His own image, in the image of God He created him; male and female He created them.

It is hard for me to think of myself as created in His image, as God is my husband and thus a man, and I don't want to look like a man. To this day, the Lord still reminds me that I was created in His splendor. As mentioned in another chapter, He gave me Ezekiel 16:14, which has a very special meaning regarding how God created me.

When I think of God's splendor, I think of flowers, flowering trees, a beautiful sunset, even a squirrel eating an acorn, things God created which I find beautiful and would love to be likened to. When I was married, my husband only ever said two things that made me feel good about myself. The day we were married, he told me I was beautiful, and he would tell me my eyes were beautiful when I cried. I do recall my gentleman friend telling me he loved taking me out to dinner because when men would look at me, he was the one by my side, not them. Perhaps it was my pride and desire to be flattered, especially since I rarely noticed when men looked at me, but the comment came from his heart and it gave me a sense of self-worth.

Men may look, but rarely do they talk to me. I have been told by men and women alike that I can be intimidating. What God showed me was Isaiah 32:17, which says:

> The fruit of righteousness will be peace; the effect of righteousness will be quietness and confidence forever. (NIV)

Additionally, Jeremiah 17:7 says:

> "But blessed is the man who trusts in the LORD, whose confidence is in him. (NIV)

I am confident because I know the Lord God Almighty, and no other reason. Those who know me well know that I am a simple, childlike woman who fears the Lord. To fear God means to reverence Him; it doesn't mean to be afraid of Him. Job 4:6 says:

> "Is not your fear of God your confidence, And the integrity of your ways your hope?

With God, we can walk in confidence, which is how I chose to live.

This was best stated by a man who attended the church. He once asked me, "Have you ever thought that the reason men don't approach you is because God is saving you for your husband?" That question was liberating. I was reminded of the time the pastor said from the pulpit, "I don't want the woman God has for me to be friends with a lot of men." Well, that sure described me. But at the same time, I wondered why Pastor made no attempt to talk to me. That sure didn't help my self-esteem.

Actually, we both tried initiating conversations, but they went nowhere. I determined it was in God's timing, and that He would bring us to our destinies. It was no easy task to have faith in this God-appointed marriage, especially since there was such a spiritual battle involved. Although it could be perceived as prideful on my part, I must admit that it made me feel good to have my ex-husband and gentlemen friend try to come back into my life. Of course, those doors were closed, but it was flattering to know that they wanted me back in their lives.

At least, that is what each of them told me. I determined that if they really wanted me back in their lives, my gentleman friend would have to attend the church I attended, and my ex would need to go to church in Tucson, read the Word, and seek God's face. But, I never heard any mention from either of them about wanting to know God on a personal or closer level, so I knew they were not to be in my life.

Rejection was the biggest enemy Pastor battled. From my earliest recollection of attending the church, I saw the spirit of rejection on him.

I knew it well – how it manifests and operates, as I was married to a man and had a gentleman friend who both battled the same spirit. It manifested itself differently in each man, but interestingly, both manifestations revealed themselves in and through the pastor. The gentleman friend drew me and other women close to him, and would then close the door after a period of time. Rejection manifested itself in my ex-husband as anger. Being surrounded by rejection for eighteen years gave me insight into the pastor and the battle he was facing. As he shared his personal life from the pulpit, I heard many similarities between the three men.

Only by the grace of God was I able to endure my ex's anger for as long as I did. Or perhaps it was my innocence of never acknowledging the enemy in him. Usually, I ignored the anger and kept moving forward. As Proverbs 26:20 states:

> For lack of wood the fire goes out; And where there is no whisperer, contention quiets down.

Or, as I like to paraphrase the proverb, where there is no fuel, there is no fire. If I didn't engage in the battle, it would die out. That is how I lived my life with an angry man for twelve years.

His rejection resulted from a variety of things that happened in his life. For one thing, my ex-husband never knew his father. He only saw him from a distance on three separate occasions and was raised by numerous aunts. Additionally, his mother had great animosity toward him because he closely resembled his father. However, I think the biggest reason for his feelings of rejection was a young woman whom he met and fell in love with while in medical school in Mexico City. She was from a prominent Mexican family, and he was from Sinaloa, a northern state in Mexico. From what I understood about the culture of the country, citizens of Mexico City look down upon those from the northern states. As a result, the young woman was told by her family to dump the medical doctor or risk losing everything – and so she did just that.

Add to this the fact that his first wife cheated on him. I believe he determined at that point that no woman was going to hurt him again. Thus, when he met me, he already had it in his mind that he was not going to let any woman ever love him again. The best way to receive no love is to reject the person who tries to love you. But he didn't expect to meet and marry a woman who loves the Lord with all her heart.

The love I have for Jesus enabled me to love my husband too, right where he was, unconditionally. Just like Jesus tells us in Luke 10:27:

> And he answered, "YOU SHALL LOVE THE LORD YOUR GOD WITH ALL YOUR HEART, AND WITH ALL YOUR SOUL, AND WITH ALL YOUR STRENGTH, AND WITH ALL YOUR MIND; AND YOUR NEIGHBOR AS YOURSELF."

Ultimately, my ex knows he messed up. I loved him, prayed for him and his salvation, and was the Godly wife I was called to be to him. He either couldn't receive my love or he chose not to receive it – I don't know which; maybe it was both. Either way, it was his free will that determined how he treated me.

Through the gentleman friend, rejection revealed itself in his drawing in and cutting off of the women in his life, what I refer to as passive-aggressive behavior. He would be in my life for about a year; then he would leave and not contact me for long periods of time, before returning again. Each time I let him back in. For whatever reason, he kept coming back into my life, and with each return he became more emotionally attached, opening up to me about his life. He never returned to the other women he drew in and dropped. I know this, as he used to talk with me about his actions. He would comment that I was different from the other women. I believe it was Jesus in me that kept drawing him back to our friendship. I never closed the door to him, loved him where he was, and never asked for more than he could give me emotionally. It wasn't until God closed the door that I closed it, too.

In my earliest years attending the church, Pastor tried numerous times to get to know me, but I kept asking God, "What is this?" When given the revelation, a spirit of rejection, I knew exactly how to handle the situation. I was to love him right where he was, and not engage in the eye contact he used with so many women in church. I sat in the congregation for three years, watching, listening, and praying. I would not let him draw me in so he could cut me off at some point in the future.

It was amazing to watch God work in the pastor's life. The rejection was still present, but over time and with my patience and love for a man who was trying to reject me, the negative spirit began to dissipate. It took time and perseverance on both of our parts, but Pastor came to realize that I wasn't moving or giving up on him. I was able to withstand the enemy. I never rejected my ex-husband or my gentleman friend, and I wasn't going to reject the pastor, either, even though each of them had rejected me in one way or another.

Eventually the pastor learned that I never rejected him, and God was taking him to a place where he would know, without a shadow of a doubt, that I would always be there for him, regardless of how angry he was with me. As he once said from the pulpit, "Sometimes you just have to outlast the enemy," which is exactly what I did. Praise God! As Proverbs 27:17 says:

> Iron sharpens iron, So one man sharpens another.

This best describes what God was doing in each of us. We were delivered from our bad character, and we were sharpening each other. Even if we didn't realize it at the time, we were knocking the burrs off the iron rod until we were smooth and ready for each other.

God is so faithful and gracious as He heals us of our hurts. For whatever reason, God has given me a very forgiving and loving heart. It is a gift for which I thank Him. Through all of these situations, I never harbored ill will or thoughts toward the pastor, only love. Although I was outlasting the enemy, I knew my presence was also a hindrance to the pastor's deliverance from rejection. I didn't know how or what was going to happen, but I knew that as time passed, he wasn't getting to the place God wanted him to be. It wasn't until we talked in October and I stepped away from the church for a season that I believe his deliverance occurred and I was healed of hurts I hadn't even known existed.

We each needed deliverance from our character flaws; otherwise we were going to continually hurt each other and others in the congregation, just as he had preached on several occasions. I was now beginning to understand why it was taking so long for God to put us together.

CHAPTER 15

One Final Instruction

During the same ten-day fast from television mentioned previously, the Lord spoke and told me to start writing. OK. I had a pen and paper, so I started to write – thoughts, scriptures, and words He was speaking to me. I never questioned the command. I worked with what I had, pen and paper. Shortly after I began to write, I was blessed with a computer. I didn't ask for it, it just showed up the Sunday that the pastor told me not to shake his hand or write him anymore notes. It was a blessing, a gift, for the persecution I'd endured from the pastor, but it was also the setup for my future.

Shortly after receiving the computer, God spoke and said, "Write the testimony of how I put the marriage together." I started to write in early September. I finished the first draft at the end of the same month. The morning after I completed the first draft, the Lord spoke, "I have a very specific instruction for you. I will surround you and protect you. Give Mama and Papa a copy of the book. I will confirm it. They won't read it, but give it to the pastor. As he reads it, he will see and learn who you are."

Knowing what happened with each of the three notes, I was hesitant to do it, but by the time I received my confirmation, I knew the draft would be ready to give to them. My written confirmation came the next day while on the train. I opened the Bible by faith and received 1 Samuel, Chapter 15. Saul was disobedient to an instruction given to him by God. 1 Samuel 15:22-23 states it best:

> Samuel said, "... Behold, to obey is better than sacrifice, And to heed than the fat of rams. For rebellion is as the sin of divination, And insubordination is as iniquity and idolatry. ..."

Since confirmation in the Word came so quickly, I decided to wait for confirmation from the pulpit. That confirmation came the second Tuesday in October, when the pastor said, "There are books to be written." God's instruction was now confirmed by both the Word and from the pulpit.

The second Saturday in October, I took the draft manuscript to church. God moved that night, and I wept before and during the service. I was being asked to follow an instruction, and based on previous experiences, the reception wasn't going to be warm and fuzzy. I had to trust that God would protect and surround me as He said he would. While working in the bookstore, I began to weep. A woman approached me and asked, "What's the matter?"

I responded, "I walk a very difficult walk." I was going to give the book to Mama, and I had no idea how it was going to be received. The woman who asked the question didn't understand, but I didn't expect her to. Not many people would be or are willing to walk in the obedience I have been asked to walk in; but I said yes to God's call, no matter the cost.

During service, God spoke to me and said, "I'm birthing something in you, *get ready.*" I went up to the altar and started to pray Romans, Chapter 1 over the pulpit. I prayed God's radiance would permeate the sanctuary and people would be drawn from all over the city to the service on Sunday and that salvations would take place. While I prayed, I heard the pastor say something. I had to watch the service the next day on the Internet to learn what he had said. Out of his mouth had come Isaiah 54:17. I believe he thought the prayer I was praying, even though I don't think he could hear me, was against him. It wasn't. The scripture says:

> "No weapon that is formed against you will prosper...

While watching the video of the service, I noticed that Papa stood on the platform in front of me and listened to what I prayed. He knew I wasn't praying anything against the pastor; my prayers were only positive things for the church.

Having prayed, I returned to my seat and waited for direction from the Lord to give Mama the book. When I handed her the book, she looked at me, as if to ask, "Why are you doing this?"

I explained, "It was an instruction from the Lord."

Having been home only a few minutes, my cell phone rang. It was the pastor. I greeted him with a cheerful voice, and then it happened – a conversation I wasn't prepared for. He asked if I had given the envelope to his mother, and I agreed that I had. Then he asked, "Didn't you realize that giving the book to my mom was like giving it to me?"

I thought, "Yes, as God already told me the book would go to you, but I didn't think it would happen so quickly." He then proceeded to suggest I start attending another church. I questioned him, "Aren't churches open to anyone?"

"Yes," he responded, and then proceeded to tell me that I had not been hearing from God.

I was not argumentative and admitted, "Well, it wouldn't be the first time." We all make mistakes, and giving the draft book to his mother wouldn't be the first time I'd heard a message incorrectly; but honestly, I was sure I'd heard it from God, as I had received confirmations. Then the pastor alluded that the church leadership was considering placing a restraining order against me.

WOW! I was speechless. In that instant, I remembered placing a restraining order against my ex-husband, and I backed down. I couldn't believe it, to think that the leadership saw me as threatening, when all I had done was follow God's instructions. The purpose of the draft book was to help the pastor get to the place where God wanted him to be and to know me. I told the pastor I would honor his request. My response made him realize I was agreeing to step away from the church, and he then tried to start a conversation about my boldness. Acknowledging his statement and my boldness, I said, "Yes." I thought to myself, "I'm bold because God asks it of me," and I reiterated that I would honor his request.

Realizing what just transpired, he said "OK," and hung up the phone.

I got off the phone and asked the Lord, "What just happened?" How could I get the instruction wrong again? And why had the pastor reacted to the circumstance, instead of seeking God's face for an answer or direction? The Holy Spirit prompted me to open the Bible. I received Luke 10:11:

> *Even the dust of your city which clings to our feet we wipe off in protest against you; yet be sure of this, that the kingdom of God has come near.*

Then the Spirit prompted me to open the Word again. This time I received Genesis 37, the story about Joseph going from the pit to the palace. This was the first time I had ever received that story when opening the Word by faith. God spoke to me, "You have a choice."

I replied, "I want to do Your will," and started to pray. Having fasted my Saturday evening meal, I continued my fast until late Sunday afternoon. As I prayed and fasted, God began to show me His will, and I was led to draft an email to the church leadership that afternoon.

The first thing He brought to my mind was the women in church whom He had placed in my path to minister. God was using me to encourage, pray, or share a word of knowledge with these women. They knew they could trust me and would share personal information with me in confidence. Then He showed me the woman I was to give a ride to for the upcoming women's Bible study. At that point, I said to the Lord, "I want to return to church." I knew it was His will for me to return; otherwise, He would have shown me something different. I didn't want to miss out on what He had for me, but He gave me a choice.

I believed the pastor was my husband. I was not going to be the one who closed the door. If the door was going to close, it would have to come from him. So I wrote the following email to the leadership:

Dear Church Leadership –

Since my conversation with pastor, I have been in prayer and fasting all last night and day. First, asking God to forgive me for the mistakes I have made toward you all – you know what they are (though I'm sure there are things that I am unaware of, above and beyond what I know). He is a forgiving God, and I hope that you, too, can forgive me.

We all sin and fall short of the glory of God, but He is gracious and merciful. I hope that you will show me the grace and mercy that He does.

I know I said to Pastor that I would honor his request of not attending church, but it is in my heart that I would be falling right into the enemy's trap to do so, to take me out of the place and assignment that God has called me to.

I understand that it may take time to restore your confidence in me, but know that I always do what I believe God is telling me, and that includes doing things that require great boldness. Boldness is part of my walk, although I don't have a full understanding of it, yet. Because I fear the Lord, I do what He asks of me in faith. Repercussions from man or not, it is God who establishes me.

Honestly, when I heard the instruction to give the book to Papa and Mama, it did not occur to me that it would be like giving it to Pastor. I see them as separates, not as one. I guess that's where the wiles of the enemy came in to stir things up, and he did. Lesson learned.

And if I am doing what I believe God has required of me and it wasn't Him, then I have to stand (and I am standing) on His Word. For it says in Romans 8:28, "And we know that in all things God works for the good of those who love him, who have been called according to his purpose."

God knows my heart and motive in every situation. Even David failed miserably on occasion (Bathsheba comes to mind), but God still used him in a mighty way.

Please forgive me and know that I will be attending church going forward. A righteous man falls seven times, but gets back up. I'm getting back up!

Julie

On Monday evening, I received a phone call from the children's ministry leader, who also happens to be the pastor's cousin. She talked and I listened for most of the conversation, except for me saying that I appreciated her phone call. The outcome of the call was that each party would take a break for a season. I was not to contact the church; they would contact me. I agreed. At least the door was not closed on either party's part. So as far as I was concerned, the enemy didn't have a foothold on the pastor, the church, or me.

Before the phone call from church, I was talking to a friend about what had happened over the weekend. As we talked, she prayed that it was now up to the pastor to do anything, going forward, as I had done all God had required of me. I called my friend back after my conversation with the cousin, and she reminded me, "Absence makes the heart grow fonder." Now, to trust God about how long the season was going to last!

For the first few days, I prayed and gave thanks. By Wednesday, though, I started to question how I could have been so wrong in hearing His voice and what had prompted me to honor the pastor's request to find another church. As I prayed, the comment about the restraining order came to mind. Immediately, memories of my marriage started to flood my mind: I had to place a restraining order on my ex-husband because he was a threat to my life.

The bad memories of my first marriage began to surface, and I realized that I had suppressed *a lot* of stuff. I just cried. I thought to myself, "How could the leadership think I was a threat to the pastor?" It just didn't make sense.

Anyone with whom I shared the story of what had happened said the same thing: "They don't know you; if they did, they would never say such a thing."

Needless to say, I was devastated and it took weeks for me to recuperate from the statement. These were people I loved and to whom I gave my heart, and they were telling the pastor that I was a threat to his life. All I could do was pray for them and the ringleader. I couldn't understand how this person – or people – could plant such a negative seed in his mind. Maybe the leadership never actually said those fateful words, but I believe someone said something negative about me to him. The enemy is a liar! But, where was the pastor's discernment in the situation? Not only did he react to the draft book, but he was listening to someone who, because of my obedience to God, thought I was a threat to him.

Each of the instructions I followed were always vindicated from the pulpit. Even if no one else knew, the pastor and I did. I continued to pray for whoever thought I was a threat. At the same time, God started to stir in me. As the past began to surface, it became obvious that wounds I had thought were healed weren't. Within the first two weeks of the comment, all the pain from the men who had hurt me were addressed: I was reminded that the old boyfriend I'd caught cheating on me with another woman had died unexpectedly; I had the strength to not engage with the gentleman friend who'd walked out and tried returning on a few separate occasions; and my dad passed away. Then there was my ex-husband. I thought I was healed of the verbal, emotional, and psychological abuse I had endured for twelve years, but I wasn't.

What I initially thought was going to be a two-week process of healing from the abuse of my ex-husband turned into six months. Every time I thought the process was finished, God brought someone else into my path to share my testimony. Each time I shared, I cried tears of cleansing and healing. I cried for days, weeks, and months. What a healing! God had to open the wound so He could cleanse it and then heal it properly. Anyone who had known my ex and me as a couple acknowledged how poorly I had been treated. But as I continued to share my testimony, God used each instance for my benefit.

Can anything happen without the Lord's permission?
Lamentations 3:37 (NLT)

I was devastated at the time, but the comment about the restraining order and my time away from the church resulted in a time of healing for me. I don't know what God was doing in the pastor simultaneously. The Lord led me to a place where I would be whole and He could bring me into my destiny. What seemed like a setback was actually a setup for my future.

I knew I was healed and ready to return to church, but God knows best, and He instructed me to write about my experiences during this time. So, actually one final instruction turned into two! I would not return until I had finished writing about what transpired in the six months I was away from the church.

CHAPTER 16

Lessons Learned - Great Messages

The pastor and I each went through the exposure of character flaws, hindrances, deliverances, and various instructions. With each instruction I followed, I learned a lesson. Some of the lessons were immediate, while others took nearly a year to understand. The pastor's quick reaction to each note and the draft book led to lessons that resulted in some of his best messages. Unfortunately, he received the revelation behind each situation following a conversation, not prior to one. As far as I know, the pastor, perhaps a few others, and I were the only people who knew the reason behind each message.

When you go to church, you go with the expectation of hearing the Word, a scriptural message from the pulpit you can apply to your life. The message might be a confirmation, an understanding, or an explanation of a scripture or story. In my case, the messages were vindications that either enlightened me about myself or helped me grow spiritually.

The following are some of the pastor's best messages which resulted from our sharpening each other. The Bible is full of lessons, many taught through parables in the New Testament and stories from the Old Testament. As I grow in the Lord, I learn more about how to read the Bible. It is inspired from God, as 2 Timothy 3:16 says:

All Scripture is inspired by God and profitable for teaching, for reproof, for correction, for training in righteousness;

Since the Word was written by inspiration, it should be read the same way. Expect to learn and grow. As you read the scriptures, don't just read them, but *read* them. How does what you are reading relate to your life, circumstances, situation, or a bigger picture? What are you experiencing presently in life, and how does the message apply?

Meditate on it; ask what is the message or lesson to be learned, or the point God is trying to instill in you. The answer may come immediately, or it may take time; the hope is that you will understand the lesson and grow from it. Keep moving forward. Life is a series of lessons, processes, and experiences. As I read the Bible, I share the lessons and explanations for each situation I experienced throughout the book.

The following synopses and corresponding scripture references illustrate some of the highlights from the pastor's many messages.

The Best of Times. Resistance is not always the enemy; it can be God trying to propel us to another level. This message was based on the second note I sent the pastor. I believe God was trying to deliver Pastor from something, and He used the second note to continue the process He had begun with the first note. For me, it took a year before I understood that God was using the pastor to bring me to a place of being comfortable talking to men.

The centurion didn't listen to Paul the first time, but paid attention the second time Paul spoke. The scripture references are Acts 27:9-11 and Acts 27:22-25, respectively:

> *When considerable time had passed and the voyage was now dangerous, since even the fast was already over, Paul began to admonish them, and said to them, "Men, I perceive that the voyage will certainly be with damage and great loss, not only of the cargo and the ship, but also of our lives." But the centurion was more persuaded by the pilot and the captain of the ship than by what was being said by Paul.*

"Yet now I urge you to keep up your courage, for there will be no loss of life among you, but only of the ship. For this very night an angel of the God to whom I belong and whom I serve stood before me, saying, 'Do not be afraid, Paul; you must stand before Caesar; and behold, God has granted you all those who are sailing with you.' "Therefore, keep up your courage, men, for I believe God that it will turn out exactly as I have been told.

Thank God for Your Enemies/Your Enemies Prophesy Your Promotion. Persecution is sometimes necessary to take the believer to the next level of growth, and the person cannot take it personally. Get ready to send a thank you note to those who persecuted you during the year. Little did I know that two months following this message, I would step away from the church; then six months after stepping away, my promotion occurred. The scripture reference the pastor taught from was Matthew 5:11-12, which says:

"Blessed are you when people insult you and persecute you, and falsely say all kinds of evil against you because of Me. Rejoice and be glad, for your reward in heaven is great; for in the same way they persecuted the prophets who were before you.

Renewing Our Minds. If you want to know what God is telling or guiding you to do, get connected with the Word of God. Confusion will flee when we read the Word. If you are unsure of what God is instructing you to do, renew your mind by reading the Bible and wait on the Lord until you have peace. The scripture references for this message was Romans 12:2. It says:

And do not be conformed to this world, but be transformed by the renewing of your mind, so that you may prove what the will of God is, that which is good and acceptable and perfect.

But, it is also important to know that God will give you peace when following His instructions.

for God is not a God of confusion, but of peace ...
1 Corinthians 14:33

Prayer & Worship. The pastor revisited a teaching he had preached a while back. It was based on praise and worship and the spiritual and natural shaking that takes place while doing it. God was shaking us up in our own respective areas to prepare what He had in store. My natural shaking came when I repainted and rearranged my bedroom and living room. That natural shaking was the beginning of a spiritual shaking that lasted more than a year and was the prelude to things to come leading to my destiny. The scripture to support the events was Acts 16:25-26:

About midnight Paul and Silas were praying and singing hymns to God, and the other prisoners were listening to them. Suddenly there was such a violent earthquake that the foundations of the prison were shaken. At once all the prison doors flew open, and everybody's chains came loose. (NIV)

The Keys to Your Walls Coming Down. Instruction always precedes the incredible miracle. Follow God's instructions. I followed the instruction to give the book to Mama and Papa. They immediately gave it to Pastor, which led to his walls coming down, as well as my own. Mission accomplished! The pastor referenced Joshua, Chapter 6, and the story of walking around the walls of Jericho.

Put Down the Rock. Moses was following instructions from God in an effort to get the Israelites to the place God had for them, but all they wanted to do was stone him. In this message, the pastor preached how the person who loves you the most is the one who is willing to tell you what you don't want to hear. Put down the rock! The entire story is found in Exodus, Chapter 17, with emphasis given to Exodus 17:4:

> So Moses cried out to the LORD, saying, "What shall I do to this people? A little more and they will stone me."

With each message, the pastor was being transformed. If I saw the positive change while attending church and then watching online, surely the congregation noticed, too. His preaching, which once seemed to have an element of anger and intensity, was now becoming filled with love and gentleness. He was humble and able to preach the message without yelling and screaming. It was different, and I watched him grow.

For me, the messages were not only of vindication, but of growth. Some of my progress came while I attended church, but it wasn't until after I left that my real growth occurred. I can look back on the messages now and see how they helped me advance toward my destiny.

My vindication took place during my tenure and after I left the church. It came in the form of messages and public apologies; friends who still attend the church shared those public apologies with me. Not only was each public confession toward me, but they were also for others who have been offended by the church leadership over the years. I believe they were heartfelt messages and apologies. When God wants you to know something, He will be sure to get the message to you.

Had the pastor contacted me, I would have told him that I'd forgiven him. Maybe the day will come and the *air will be cleared.*

CHAPTER 17

Correction and Conviction, but No Condemnation

Our fathers disciplined us for a little while as they thought best; but God disciplines us for our good, that we may share in his holiness. Hebrews 12:10 (NIV)

Like a parent disciplines their child, so does God discipline His children. Knowing the difference between correction, conviction, and discipline was key to my personal growth as a believer and to my future destiny.

Correction is defined as scolding, rebuking, or punishing in order to effect improvement. It usually is intended for a person who is out of order, at fault, or in error. I have received correction from God on many occasions over my years as a believer, but I received one correction from the pastor because of his own personal ideas, not necessarily God's. The correction came from the pulpit and dealt with being zealous for God. My zeal for the Lord and how He moves me at church and in my home makes me want to dance, shout, and just be demonstrative. Unfortunately, it took a long time for me to understand how my enthusiasm for the Lord could have a negative effect on others, especially new believers or those attending church, including the pastor. Many people are unaccustomed to how God can move through individuals or a congregation in a Spirit-filled church.

For many months, the pastor would occasionally say, "Don't be weird." I knew he was talking to me, as I would become very expressive when the Spirit of the Lord came upon me. Honestly, I didn't care, as God is the One who establishes me and I love to dance before the Lord, whether in my house or at church. But the pastor regularly made comments from the pulpit about being weird. I took it to the Lord, and He showed me Proverbs 12:4:

> An excellent wife is the crown of her husband, But she who shames him is like rottenness in his bones.

I knew God was showing me that the zeal I had for Him was not pleasing to the pastor, so I asked the Lord to help me. I was fine to squelch my zeal for a while, but I would eventually become enthusiastic again. Then one day I read 2 Samuel 6:16, 23:

> Then it happened as the ark of the LORD came into the city of David that Michal the daughter of Saul looked out of the window and saw King David leaping and dancing before the LORD; and she despised him in her heart.
>
> Michal, the daughter of Saul had no child to the day of her death.

This scripture showed me that my zeal for dancing before the Lord was pleasing in His eyes, and it was confirmed by the Greek pastor, who mentioned this scripture in a message he preached. His message was actually for the pastor: "It's OK that she dances. Pastor, you may not get a wife if you're so upset with this behavior."

But it wasn't until a woman from the church said something to me that I had a complete understanding. She told me that the pastor has a congregation of people that includes new believers, some of them people who have never been to church before. He has to be careful so that people who are unaccustomed to the ways the Spirit of the Lord moves (e.g., my zeal) aren't turned off. Through her, the Lord showed me that I could not be so demonstrative as a pastor's wife. I needed to keep my zeal under control, yet still allow the power of God to use me. I finally understood what the pastor had been saying from the pulpit since February.

As we spoke, the woman said that because I was willing to humble myself and not be puffed up (i.e., I took the correction), God could now use me accordingly. It was dross, not loss that God was removing. I am so grateful for this lesson. At first, I had the knowledge, but not the understanding. Now, I had the understanding to accompany the revelation and knowledge. God was using me as I stood in place while praying and praising Him.

This was an area where compromise would be necessary. I could dance, but not crazily, and the pastor would simply have to accept this as one of my idiosyncrasies. Ultimately, God vindicated me when the following word was spoken over me at the new church I began attending. The man of God prophesied:

You are a worshiper, you are a worshiper, you are a worshiper...
He says, "You have freedom here to be yourself and just worship
Me. Because as you be yourself in Me, I will be Myself in you.
Hallelujah."

This prophetic word told me that my zeal for the Lord was beautiful in His eyes.

I cannot hide who God has created me to be in Him. The lesson I learned: *Be unafraid to dance, shout, sing, or play an instrument before the Lord, as it is well pleasing to Him and it is scriptural. Don't worry what others think; keep your eyes on Him. Everyone has his or her own idea about how to glorify the Lord, but their ideas should not influence how each of us praise and worship Him.*

The purpose of conviction is to prove or declare one guilty of an offense. An offense to God is a violation or breaking of His laws, a transgression, or a sin. Conviction comes from the Holy Spirit and no one else, but the Holy Spirit can use a person to bring the conviction of the wrongdoing. Most of my convictions were not immediate, but came from circumstances that caused a stirring in me about an issue. One of the most profound convictions came about eight years after my divorce, when God dealt with me about prioritizing my then-husband behind my work. God is omniscient, all knowing, and He knows the perfect time to address an action or statement. Confess it and move on. As 1 John 1:9 says:

> *If we confess our sins, he is faithful and just and will forgive us our sins and purify us from all unrighteousness.* (NIV)

The key to being disciplined is the willingness to accept it. It is in our own best interest to do so. If we will decrease and move our humanness and pride out of the way, God can really come in and do what He wants to do. He can take us to the place He has for us. If we are unwilling, then He cannot do what He has destined for each of us. He gives us free will. Are we willing to accept the chastisement and learn from the lesson, or will we refuse it and stay where we are spiritually? Personally, I will take the discipline and request that I learn the lesson quickly so I can move forward.

When I do not understand what is going on around me and I see the same thing happening again and again, I ask the Lord, "What is the lesson I am supposed to be learning?" For me, becoming the pastor's wife meant I had to be willing to accept direction from the pastor, whether from the pulpit or in person. He is the Shepherd of the Church, and I believed to be the head of my household, so I needed to trust that God would use him to guide me and the congregation in the direction that was best for everyone.

This is not to say that when discipline comes from someone, I won't take it to the Lord in prayer. Ultimately, correction should be confirmed; in the case of my zeal for God, it was spoken many times by the pastor, and it was also confirmed by the written Word with regards to the pastor's idea of how an *excellent wife* should behave. But the Greek pastor said it was OK to dance, as does the Word of God. The comments from the pulpit may have been unwarranted; perhaps God was using me to help the pastor get over his own ideas about how his wife should behave and for me to learn how to submit to spiritual and natural authority.

Condemnation can be defined as judgment or disapproval of an action or comment. Do not let any person, your mind, or the spiritual enemy tell you that you have not been forgiven once the circumstance is confessed. In my situation, the enemy *tried* to use the pastor to condemn me by telling me that I could not be weird in church. A trick of the enemy is to try to tell us that the behavior is not forgiven or is unacceptable and to continue to remind us of it, using shame and remembrance as the vehicles to condemn. You always know it's the enemy making you feel bad or condemned, because he continues to repeat the same message again and again.

Condemnation comes from the enemy, not from God. As Romans 8:1 states:

> *Therefore there is now no condemnation for those who are in Christ Jesus.*

This is one of the first promises I believed when I first became a Christian. I spoke the scripture out loud, meditated on it, and trusted the Word. My believing the promise resulted in very little condemnation over the years, but when the enemy tried to condemn me, it usually had to do with my job. During the season when I was making mistakes at work, thoughts would enter my mind that I was going to lose my job. One thing to know about God is that everything happens in His time, so the words related to losing my job were not of God, and consciously, I knew this. That didn't stop the mental attacks, so I stood on His promise, His Word. I couldn't look at the circumstances or the facts, because in the natural, it looked as if I *was* going to lose my job.

God is faithful, and as I persevered through the various scenarios presented to me, I trusted His Word, knowing there is no condemnation for those who are in Christ Jesus. According to John 10:10:

> "The thief comes only to steal and kill and destroy; I came that they may have life, and have it abundantly.

The enemy (i.e., the thief) tried to condemn me, to steal my joy for honest mistakes both in church and at work. I took responsibility for my actions, but the enemy tried to use others to continue to bring those circumstances up and throw them in my face. The enemy would like nothing more than to cause God's destiny for me to go unaccomplished. I remained unshakable, held my head high, and *stood* on His promises knowing that God alone establishes me. Understanding this simple principle allows each of us to walk in the freedom into which He has called us and brings us closer to our destiny.

CHAPTER 18

Trials and Tribulations

Trials and tribulations are a part of life. How we handle the situations tends to determine how often we will experience them. Through all the trials I have faced over my life as a born-again Christian, I have chosen to live by the following scripture in James 1:2:

Consider it all joy, my brethren, when you encounter various trials,

I learned early on that the more quickly I walked through the trial, rather than around it, the more quickly I learned the lesson and was able to move forward. God will use unfortunate circumstances in our life with the intention of building our character. Being able to rejoice, persevere, have peace, and be grateful for the lesson can be quite difficult, but overcoming the situation has great rewards and always brought me closer to my destiny.

Some of my trials and tribulations came in the workplace. Whether it was a supervisor who set me up to fail, or other circumstances, the trial amidst the adversity always drew me closer to God. As I walked through each furnace put before me, it became easier each time – so much easier that I actually began to walk in unshakable faith, knowing the resolution would come and it would be positive. One of the most profound tribulations came about via my job at a state university. At one point in my career, I began to make mistakes. Simple tasks I'd always known were now errors. Forgetting procedures and practices on a regular basis, I felt I was losing my mind, both literally and figuratively. The mistakes became so prevalent that my authorities, placed me on an unofficial performance review.

All I could do was acknowledge the mistakes I made and keep praying that God would get me through the situation. This process, from beginning to end, lasted from seven to ten months; I don't even recall how long, as I lived for the day. I prayed, asking God to renew my mind. I began daily to pray to align my thought process with God's Word, as it is written in Romans 12:2:

> *And do not be conformed to this world, but be transformed by the renewing of your mind, so that you may prove what the will of God is, that which is good and acceptable and perfect.*

The experience is best described by the Ephesians 6:12, which states:

> *For our struggle is not of flesh and blood, but against the rulers, against the powers, against the world forces of this darkness, against the spiritual forces of wickedness in the heavenly places.*

Nevertheless, it was a painful ordeal, and at one point, I began looking for another job at the university. Every time I applied for a position, some type of computer glitch occurred, which led to either a wrong or incomplete application being uploaded into the human resource system. I don't think all of it was my doing. This wasn't exactly new, as I was initially hired for a position for which I never applied. God set things up for my benefit. It was a computer glitch that placed me on my career path at the university in the first place, and I believe it was another glitch that kept me from moving into a different position. God placed me in my current position for a reason, and the lesson was about withstanding trials and tribulations.

I remember God asking me a few times during this period of duress,

"What do you want? Do you want a career that pays more? I will still use you and take you to the top of your profession. Or do you want to do My will?" This I knew to be a Pastor's wife in full-time ministry.

I remember saying to Him, "Lord, I want Your will for me."

At that point, I needed the grace to get through the adversity I was encountering at work. I wrote the following scripture on my whiteboard at work and began to stand on Isaiah 7:7:

thus says the Lord GOD: "It shall not stand nor shall it come to pass.

Anything the enemy was trying to place in my path was not going to happen. God would prevail; I trusted in His promise. I was able to share this scripture with other women who were experiencing trials and tribulations at work, as well. They knew what I'd endured and survived; now these same women were coming to me for prayer.

The interesting thing is that while I was having problems at work, I was also experiencing scrutiny from the leadership at church. Anything I said or did, even if it was an instruction from the Lord, was questioned. I had to weather this storm too. He placed me in the eye of the storm where it is calm and I could rest and trust in Him. I could spiritually see the mess going on around me, but through it all, I remained in the presence of God and the peace that surpasses all understanding.

Between my workplace and church, the scrutiny was fierce. I remember crying at church one Sunday, and a well-respected female elder asked me, "What's the matter?" I told her I was at my wits' end with the scrutiny.

When she asked me if it was coming from work, I responded, "Yes, but also from church." She asked who was judging me, and I replied, "It doesn't matter." At that point, I dropped the subject, and so did she.

With God's guidance, grace, and mercy I survived the situations at work and at church. The tears were a spiritual cleansing. The same elder asked me the following week how I was doing, and I explained, "It was a cleansing." She asked if I'd had a headache afterward. I replied that I had not. She then told me that if the tears had been of the flesh, I would have had a headache. I'd never heard that before, so I believe it truly was a spiritual cleansing. After the tears, matters got better for me, both at church and at work.

Toward the end of the ordeal and scrutiny, God showed me that the tribulations I had undergone were nothing compared to what I would undergo in the ministry. I needed to *buck up*, as the pastor would say, and get accustomed to it. I didn't report to the world, but I reported to God; He is the One who establishes me and He would take me to the destination. I received Haggai 2:5 to support what He spoke to me:

> As for the promise which I made you when you came out of Egypt, My Spirit is abiding in your midst; do not fear!

I persevered, and my character was built even further. I climbed the mountain in front of me, going through the trial, instead of around it. Had I not persevered for all those months, I wouldn't be where I am today. I would be experiencing the situation again, as He gives us many opportunities to get it right. Better to endure it once, than experience the lesson multiple times, is my personal motto.

The furnace, or the major trials, became easier to handle and eventually became a refining fire; the dross needed to be addressed. About six months after coming through the furnace, I found myself in a refining fire that lasted three weeks. It was a debacle from the start, and it only got worse as time progressed. How I handled the pressure, resolved the problem, and took responsibility were all part of the refinement. Partly my fault and partly the fault of others I worked under pressure and came up with a resolution, but the problem persisted – and so did the blame. How I handled this test would show the consistency of my character. Would I take responsibility for my actions? Yes. Would I continue to walk in peace and not react to the continual shame? Yes. I remember telling a friend, "When I supervised, I brought up the problem once and never again." Any person with a conscience knows when they've erred; there is no need to continually revisit the mistake. It is their responsibility to fix it, and if they needed my assistance, I was there to support them.

I withstood the scrutiny one more time. Just when I thought it was over, another incident occurred a few days later. But this time, it was not only a refining test, but I recognized it as an attack from the enemy because the incident was no fault of my own. By the grace of God, I persevered and withstood the attacks, realizing a refining fire was bringing me to a place of character-building and love. As Zechariah 13:9 says:

> "And I will bring the third part through the fire, Refine them as silver is refined, And test them as gold is tested. They will call on My name, And I will answer them; I will say, 'They are My people,' And they will say, 'The LORD is my God.'"

The story about the woman with the issue of blood comes to mind, from Mark 5:25-34. The woman first took responsibility for her action of touching Jesus' garment, and then it was her faith that healed her. I took responsibility for my mistakes, and now I trusted that God would heal the situation at work, which would lead me to getting back in the good graces of those in authority.

When the situation was finally resolved, I cried tears of cleansing, releasing the pressure that I'd survived. God spoke to me as I wept, saying, "It's over." I knew everything was OK, and that the spiritual battle was finally finished, He could now accomplish my next steps toward my destiny. It was one last battle before God moved me into the next season. I knew it was true, when about one hour later, a friend posted the following comment on her social media page.

Step up, for you are next, whether others understand it or not! I just want to encourage someone today. While in prayer and meditation, I heard these words ... forsake the misery of the past for what you know God has shown is your future. Though you were made to seem foolish ... nothing will ever exceed "God-inspired knowing". Vindication is of the Lord, as well as elevation. Step up ... it's your turn now.

One final refining episode took place about two weeks after the first refinement. This time, not only did I walk in peace, but I kept my mouth shut, except to tell my supervisor:

> *"For nothing is hidden, except to be revealed; nor has anything been secret, but that it would come to light.* Mark 4:22

When the problem was revealed, I never said a word and only listened. I was walking in Christ-like character, and I passed the test!

Furnaces and refining fires need to occur. They can be used to build our character, further refine our character, serve as discipline or as a test of our hearts, and they keep us humble. It is not comfortable to experience them, but it sure feels good when they are over. The word *overcomer* comes to mind. Stay in the fire, no matter how long it takes to overcome it. In the long run, it is a beneficial part of the process to reach your destiny. There is victory on the other side, and I now walk in it. It is my turn now!

CHAPTER 19

Doubt

A supernatural breakthrough came in early August. What started out as doubt turned out to be a turning point in my faith walk with God. The Lord brought to my mind Isaiah 59:1, the word Papa had spoken to the congregation a few days earlier. As I meditated on the spoken word, I looked up the following cross-referenced scriptures: Numbers 11:23, Ezekiel 12:25, and Habakkuk 2:3. They all talk about fulfilling the word God speaks through the prophets.

Meditating on the scriptures, I was enveloped by what I thought was the Holy Spirit, although it turned out to be a counterfeit. The thought that came to me was that the pastor was *not* my husband. The thought was confirmed when I opened my Bible by faith and received Ezekiel 44:2:

> The LORD said to me, "This gate is to remain shut. It must not be opened; no one may enter through it. It is to remain shut because the LORD, the God of Israel, has entered through it. (NIV)

I called a friend and left a message, explaining that I believed God had just shut the door on a faith walk of two years. I told my friend that it must have been the pastor's choice for the promise to end, accepting it with peace.

Then I thought, "I have a peace. Why?" Why was I doubting a promise God had given me? As Numbers 23:19 states:

> *God is not a man, that He should lie, Nor a son of man, that He should repent; Has He said, and will He not do it? Or has He spoken, and will He not make it good?*

Based on the fact that God does not lie, I repented my sin of doubt, even if only five to ten minutes. I prayed on the train from work, and when I arrived home, I knelt at my bedside and asked God to forgive me of my doubt. The Lord showed me Matthew 26:34, where Peter denied Christ three times before the cock crowed. This was a defining moment, as I had never doubted God and His instruction or direction for my life.

Like Peter, I became remorseful. I asked for forgiveness and read the Word. God showed me that even though Peter denied Christ, the Lord spoke to Him and said,

> *"I also say to you that you are Peter, and upon this rock I will build My church; and the gates of Hades will not overpower it.*
> Matthew 16:18

Standing in the kitchen and meditating on the scripture, I realized that my faith had just increased greatly – I could believe for anything and know I would receive it, as if my faith had increase by one thousand-fold. Then He brought to my mind the prayer of a friend a few days earlier: "I ask that Julie receive a thousand-fold blessing for helping me out." I understood my faith was stronger than it had ever been before. I could believe for the pastor as my husband, for the vision of the church, and for anything else that required exponential faith.

Then as further confirmation, the song "Nothing Can Ever Separate Us" came on the radio. To me, the song represented that even throughout all the situations the pastor and I had endured, nothing could separate us.

> *What therefore God has joined together, let no man separate.*
> Mark 10:9

As far as I believed, nothing could separate the pastor and me and our destiny together, unless our own free will would choose a different outcome. The enemy had been trying to place doubt in my mind ever since. I asked God to give me the discernment necessary to know the difference between the Holy Spirit and the counterfeit spirit. I had mastered the difference, but the enemy still tried to disguise himself, and I still required the awareness to know if the situation lined up with the Word of God.

Within the first few weeks of my season of waiting, I again encountered doubt. This time it wasn't the Spirit of God I doubted, it was hearing God. This time, doubt arose when the pastor told me I wasn't hearing from God during our last telephone conversation. His comment was in reference to my giving his mom the draft manuscript of this book. How could I have heard God incorrectly? Did I hear correctly when I was led to pray for something specific for someone? Doubt crept in, and I began to question everything I heard. I lost my confidence to share prophetic words with people when I received them.

After a few weeks, I decided I could not live in fear of second-guessing myself. If I made a mistake, God would work it for my benefit, as it says in Romans 8:28:

> And we know that in all things God works for the good of those who love him, who have been called according to his purpose.
> (NIV)

So one day, I stepped out in faith and sent an email to someone about a word God gave me as I prayed for them. I had received the word a few days earlier, but I needed to be sure it was God who I'd heard. As I sent the email, the Holy Spirit came upon me; it was a confirmation that I was doing the right thing. About a month later, I received a reply from the person that this person had received the word.

Opportunities began to present themselves to help me hear His voice. One incident that stands out in my mind occurred while I was on the Metro Light Rail. A disheveled man stood by the exit door where I was sitting, waiting to leave the train. I thought God said to give him some money, but I wasn't sure if it was His small, still voice or my own thought. Right before the man exited the train, he turned and looked at me with his eyes wide open. It was as if his eyes said, "Well, aren't you going to do what you are supposed to do?" Seeing the expression on his face, I knew it was God confirming that He'd been the one to speak. Not wanting to miss the instruction, I called to the man, who was now standing on the train platform and told him to come back. When he did, I handed him the money. I heard God and I received a blessing by following the instruction. Helping others out of the clear blue sky brings me great joy and blesses me.

Between these accounts and others, my confidence returned, and about the same time I was vindicated from the pulpit with regards to the book. I had heard correctly. God was trying to get the pastor to a particular place, and the book was in part the vehicle He used to get him there. Thereafter, the doubt disappeared and my faith increased. Clearly, I was back on track and nothing was going to stop me from stepping into my destiny.

CHAPTER 20

Reward

Enjoy life with the woman whom you love all the days of your fleeting life which He has given to you under the sun; for this is your reward in life and in your toil in which you have labored under the sun. Ecclesiastes 9:9

I received this scripture in November to help explain a dream I had around the same time. This was the dream:

I walked into the apartment where my husband and I lived. There was clutter everywhere. He was in the apartment, and as I began to pick up the clutter, the more I cleaned, the more the clutter accumulated. Then I went to the window, looked out, and saw a friend of his riding a bicycle in the street below. Behind the bicycle was a large open trailer with lots of stuff piled high. When I turned from the window, I saw the entire apartment filled from the floor to the ceiling with clutter.

And then I woke up. I received this interpretation: The clutter represented the spiritual and emotional baggage my husband brought to our marriage. The more I lived for Jesus (i.e., cleaned), the more the baggage exposed itself. The friend on the bicycle represented the baggage of all his friends. Between the doctor and his friends, there was so much baggage he either brought to the marriage or created while we were married that he was never unable to receive me as the reward I was to him.

The baggage included rejection, addictions and fear. With all that transpired between us verbally, emotionally and psychologically, I still forgave him. His heart toward his people was so good that God gave him a woman after His own heart. I loved him right where he was and understood why he acted the way he did toward me. Because he was unable to receive me as the reward, God allowed the divorce to take place, but not without giving him numerous opportunities to turn from his ways and repent.

I started to meditate on Ecclesiastes 9:9, the reward I was to my husband. A reward has value. A reward is something given in return for good. It can be a bonus, payment, honor, praise, or compliment to the person who is receiving the reward.

I remember one Sunday service when the pastor asked the congregation if anyone had ever been hurt. He raised his own hand, and in the Spirit, I saw the hurt he had experienced from a woman. After service, I approached him and suggested he read the same scripture. Having seen the hurt, I told him that one day, he would receive his reward. The next service, when the pastor saw me, I knew he had read the scripture, as he raised his eyes at me. I don't know if he knew I was his reward at that point, but he received the scripture. Hopefully, he meditated on the scripture and knew God only has the best for him and wouldn't give the pastor just any woman; she would truly be the reward she was called to be.

The interesting point about this whole testimony is that I have been prepared by the Lord for my assignment as a pastor's wife and for ministry. If someone would have told me in 1985, when I was first *born again,* what would be happening in my life today, I would have said they were crazy. Truly, Jeremiah 29:11 is correct:

> *For I know the plans I have for you," declares the LORD, "plans to prosper you and not to harm you, plans to give you hope and a future. (NIV)*

I am thankful I yielded to His plan. As Hebrew 11:6 states:

And without faith it is impossible to please Him, for he who comes to God must believe that He is and that He is a rewarder of those who seek Him.

I was seeking God's face continually, so I believed His Word and I, too, would be rewarded.

CHAPTER 21

Ministry

There came a point when what was taking place in the spiritual world needed to be brought into the natural. For me, it was understanding ministry. At one point, God told me that the pastor was going to be talking out of the side of his mouth; in other words, he was talking to me to give me instruction. The key for me was to understand what was being spoken to me from the pulpit and to put it into action. From the pulpit, the pastor said, "Most of what I know about ministry came from catching it, not being taught. I caught it, was not taught it."

Participating in other ministries became vital. I participated in the monthly outreach, then moved on to watching the children. An invitation to help in the bookstore was as far as my participation in ministry had gone. Early on in my attendance at the church, I was introduced to the person in charge of the bookstore and greeting ministry. At the time, I said, "Maybe I will be joining the greeters." But as soon as it came out of my mouth, both the person in charge and I knew, it wasn't going to happen. At least not then.

It took four years and the words, *caught, not taught* to come forth in a message preached by the pastor for me to understand what a call to ministry entailed. Asked to help with the greeting line on a Tuesday night, I obliged without a second thought. On Saturday of the same week, a greeter asked if I would fill the gap for her, as she would be unable to make it to church. It only took two times for me to understand that God was telling me to learn the greeting line and learn the ministry.

Standing in the greeting line allowed me to welcome, encourage, and meet members of the congregation. But one time in particular God used me with the pastor. God said, "He will be waiting by his door. You will be a confirmation to him." No other greeters had arrived and I was the only person ready to welcome people. Next thing I knew, the pastor opened up the church door and was standing outside. He turned, looked at me, and right then my spirit flipped. It was confirmation of the word God had spoken to me a few days earlier. God used me as a confirmation to the pastor about something. I asked Him to show me what I was confirming, but that was never revealed.

Sharing with a friend the events of that fateful October evening, I used the phrase "stepped away."

She said, "Don't say you have stepped away. God just spoke to me and said you are 'in between ministries.'"

At first I didn't understand the meaning behind my friend's comment, but over time, God showed me that I would be returning to the church, but in a different capacity, or at least that is what I thought. God gave me 1 Kings, Chapter 19, the scripture about Elijah running from Jezebel into the wilderness. God told Elijah to return to the wilderness of Damascus where he was to anoint others as kings and Elisha as his successor. Elijah went into the wilderness running for his life but returned to his destination with specific instructions.

Having received specific instructions about my own return, I had no idea what God's plans were for my life. My work in ministry was about to take a turn, a road less traveled, and I had no idea. I see parallels, however, to Matthew, chapters 3 and 4. At the time Jesus was water baptized by John the Baptist, he was a carpenter. After His baptism, He was led by the Spirit into the wilderness before He began His ministry. He started His life one way, but it ended differently.

While God was preparing me for ministry, the time *in between* was a time of enlightenment. The ministry would turn out to be something different from what I thought. While I waited, God began to reveal to me the mission and how the ministry would unfold. I didn't understand the following prophetic words, when spoken by the California pastor in

March, but God began to show me the meaning in His time.

I've been speaking to you about new direction and I'm going to make it really clear for you. I'm going to make it very plain on the very tablets of your heart, because God's put that in you. He's put the arts in you, He's put things in you...

Everything was lining up and in order with regard to the ministry. In the meantime, God used me in the workplace to speak scripture as opportunities arose, to speak prophetic words into people's lives and simply love them. The workplace was a ministry unto Him, and I prayed that my actions would speak the love of Jesus to those around me.

Both Elijah and Jesus spent time in the wilderness preparing for their respective assignments. The season *in between ministries* was my wilderness, and I believed my ministry would begin upon my return to the church. What transpired that night was a defining moment in my walk toward my destiny. The unexpected happened and opened doors I never would have thought possible.

> But Jesus looked at them and said to them, "With men this is impossible, but with God all things are possible."
> Matthew 19:26 (NKJV)

I was moving closer to my destiny.

CHAPTER 22

Visions and Dreams

> *... Daniel even understood all kinds of visions and dreams.*
> Daniel 1:17

I've had many visions and dreams over the years and have been given the gift of interpreting them. Recounted below are some of the visions and dreams over the past two years that involved the pastor.

The first dream actually didn't involve the pastor until it came to pass. In the dream, I saw a church service, and the Spirit of God was moving. The pastor gave an instruction for the members of the congregation to hold the hand of the person next to them. I was standing beside a gentleman, and as we held hands, the dream zoomed in on the hands. All of a sudden, God's all-consuming fire came upon me, and I woke up. I shared the dream with my girlfriend in Florida immediately.

A week later, as I left church, the pastor was standing outside the door and saw me coming. He returned to the door and shook my hand, then held it. He didn't let go, but I kept walking. As I walked, I marveled at the love generated between the two of us. I was shocked. I went home, called my girlfriend, and told her what had happened. She reminded me of the dream I'd had a week earlier, and from that time forward, I loved shaking the pastor's hand. It was always firm and sometimes lingered.

The second dream was based on the scripture "everything hidden will come to light" from Luke 12:2:

> *"But there is nothing covered up that will not be revealed, and*

hidden that will not be known.

In the dream, I walked into my mom's darkened house. I called out to see if anyone was home. From the den came a voice that was trying to disguise itself. I thought it was the pastor's, but since I wasn't sure, I backed up out of the house. Once outside, the pastor came bounding out of the house like a little kid. He kissed me quickly, then he kissed me again. My interpretation was this: What was taking place in the heavens would be revealed in the natural. The pastor was coming out of the darkness to reveal it in the light.

In the next dream, I saw myself sitting on the floor of a big box bookstore reading a magazine. As I read, the pastor came up to me on the floor, whispered in my ear, and said in reference to dating, "There is no time frame as to how long or when. This is God's will."

I whispered back into his ear, "I know," while nodding my head yes and breathing shallowly. I woke up with shallow breathing and the presence of God over me. I look back on that dream now and understand that everything that transpired over the past two years was God's timing, not ours.

Through another dream, God showed me how my guard was up with regard to the pastor. I was not to be concerned about what others thought. This was very important to understand, as God began to give me unusual directions. God establishes me, and as I do His will and obey His instructions, I cannot be concerned about what others think. Lesson learned.

Early one morning, I had a vision of a woman lying on the floor, her body limp and her head in her arms. My sense was that she had been raped multiple times by multiple men. Then God said, "YOU! You have been raped by men (not physically, but emotionally). Stand up and be strong." I believe God was telling me to keep holding my head high, and that my testimony would be used to help other women.

As I reflected on that vision in the morning, I began to cry. God has given me such love for people; I don't hold things against them. I didn't fully understand at the time, but He was preparing me for another conversation with the pastor which would lead to the opening of old wounds. Reopening these wounds would cleanse and heal me of past hurts I had suppressed, caused by my ex-husband.

Shortly before my return to the church, I dreamt about a mother and daughter driving when a tsunami covered the area and their car. After the storm passed, they got out of the car and looked at the devastation around them. All the buildings were rubble, and no other people were in the area. One said to the other, "Our faith and God's mercy kept us alive." I believe the interpretation was that I had survived the storm during the *season of waiting*.

During the same season, I had a vision. As I opened a door from outside to enter a building, the pastor was opening up the same door from the inside. At first I thought he was leaving as I was entering, but God showed me he was opening up the door to allow me to enter. However, the door he opened for me was not the same door I had interpreted. Not until the door closed at the church did I understand the dream entirely. He was opening a door that led to my destiny, of which I wasn't even yet aware.

As the time drew closer for my destiny to reveal itself, I began to dream often about giving birth and newborn babies. I was in the process of birthing something, and as much as I thought it was my husband, I didn't want to rule out any other opportunities, open doors, or ideas He had for me. I had a vision of a pair of hands holding a clock that was counting down backwards, and I understood that God was holding the clock and knew the exact time to launch me into my destiny. The same night, another vision occurred; it was a newborn cradled in a pair of arms. I knew God had me in His arms and my life all planned; all I needed to do was be obedient.

Visions and dreams are very telling, but discernment is required. Sometimes it is not easy to recognize the meaning, know whether the dream or vision is from God, or discern whether it is a message for the present or the future. Some dreams and visions are for someone other than the dreamer, and some people can interpret dreams for others, as was the case with Daniel. I have learned to be open to them, but not to place all my trust in them.

Trust God by reading and listening to the Word. He will lead and guide you and may confirm those things He is speaking to your spirit via visions and dreams.

> "'In the last days, God says, I will pour out my Spirit on all people. Your sons and daughters will prophesy, your young men will see visions, your old men will dream dreams.
> Acts 2:17 (NIV)

CHAPTER 23

Season of Waiting

The conversation between the pastor and me which led me to step away from the church for a season occurred in October. This *season of waiting* was a time I had to completely trust the Lord. This *wait* was different than any other *wait* I had experienced. When I first stepped away, I had so many questions:

> How long would the season last?
> Was the pastor still my husband?
> Why did this happen?

I received answers to all my questions during the *season of waiting*. I also received healing and understanding for past and present situations and revelation for the future.

Having removed myself from the church, I prayed and asked what was going to happen next. The first scripture God gave me was 1 Samuel 22:3:

> And David went from there to Mizpah of Moab; and he said to the king of Moab, "Please let my father and my mother come and stay with you until I know what God will do for me."

Until I know what God will do for me. In that moment, I accepted that waiting was part of God's plan. I received and stood on the scripture, and shortly thereafter, God began to move in my life.

Two days after my conversation with the pastor, I had the conversation with his cousin, during which it was agreed that I would wait until the leadership contacted me before returning to church. The door wasn't closed, but I had to trust that He would allow me to return in due season, as was discussed. I was now living in faith and trusting Him for my next chapter. As Job 14:14 states:

> "If a man dies, will he live again? All the days of my struggle I will wait Until my change comes.

When would my change come? When would the season be over? I prayed and asked in Jesus' name that it would be just four to six weeks. It wasn't.

Within my first week away from the church, God showed me that going to church had become an idol. I missed being amongst the people. I loved being of use to God, whether it was ministering to the women, praising and worshipping Him with song, or listening to His Word. Although I had been keeping my eyes on my Lord and Savior, the whole package became the draw to the church, not to God Himself. This was a conviction because it came from God, and I repented.

Immediately asking forgiveness, I didn't watch any services online for the first four weeks, at His prompting. It was just God and me. No one from church contacted me; nor were there any answers or explanations to give to anyone. It was a time God allowed so He could accomplish the things He needed to do in me. Healing from my previous marriage was the first thing He initiated. It was a healing I hadn't even known I needed, until it occurred. The process took six months and is discussed in Chapter 26, *Healing – Stay in the Process*.

At about week six, a guest preacher spoke at the church and the message was convicting. After watching the service online, I knew I would not be returning anytime soon; God was going to deal with certain people in the congregation, even though we live under grace. Kneeling, I prayed for the congregation and I found myself repenting whatever I had done wrong, even though I didn't know what it was. Convicted of my lack of reverence for the Lord God Almighty I repented of not fearing and trusting Him more, especially during this time of waiting.

About midway thru the wait, I discovered that it was, in some ways, easier to have faith for a new job than it was to have faith for the man God had chosen to be my husband and my return to the church. I had lost my job twice since becoming a believer and had moved to three different cities without a job, a place to live, or both. Actively seeking employment and collecting unemployment insurance benefits, I was taking the necessary steps to make the next chapter happen. I was living Matthew 7:7:

> "Ask and it will be given to you; seek and you will find; knock and the door will be opened to you. (NIV)

My return to church was a different story; it was totally in God's hands. There was nothing I could say or do; I was at the mercy of the church leadership, hoping they would hear from God, and when they did, that they would contact me. Although the man I believed was my husband spoke words of encouragement from the pulpit during my season away, all I could do was listen and trust in God.

Within the first few weeks of the waiting season, I asked God why I had kept my mouth shut during all of my conversations with the pastor. I received 2 Chronicles 20:17 in answer:

> 'You need not fight in this battle; station yourselves, stand and see the salvation of the LORD on your behalf, O Judah and Jerusalem.' Do not fear or be dismayed; tomorrow go out to face them, for the LORD is with you."

After meditating on the scripture, I realized I had always defended myself against my dad and my husband. They would tell me hurtful things, but I wouldn't let them talk to me in that manner. I always countered their negative comments with something positive or said something to dissipate the situation.

With the pastor, God kept my mouth shut. There was nothing I could say; the words wouldn't come out of my mouth to either defend or explain myself. I didn't understand it at first, but God was now showing me scripturally, "Julie, you don't need to defend yourself anymore – in terms of what you say or with your actions, ever again." He was saying He would fight the battle on my behalf. How liberating!

Every time my faith waned, something happened to increase it again. The more time passed, the stronger my faith became. The fact that my return seemed to be taking such a long time told me I was closer to God's promise and gave me the grace I needed to be away from the church. The word I'd spoken to the pastor a few years back came to mind: *"The longer you wait, the closer you are to your victory."* I knew, as time passed and God brought me personal victories, I was closer to returning to church and to my husband. This was now a time to trust and surrender to God's plan.

The pastor preached about this microwave society we live in, how we want things NOW. As technology increases, so does the speed of things: cooking food in microwaves, Internet access that can allow us to download information in seconds, and even automobiles and airplanes that can carry us from one destination to another quickly. Reading the Old and New Testaments shows that ancient peoples arrived at destinations on foot, cooked their food and made their offerings over fire, and sent information and goods via donkey, camel, and ship. All of those things took time. So why should I have a short faith walk and everything handed to me? Something that comes easily is not a test of faith.

As I patiently waited on the Lord, my character was being established. This gave God time to show me some areas in myself and past experiences that needed adjusting, so that I would not repeat them again. I continued to pray for my return to the church and hoped I could attend the upcoming New Year's Eve service. Yet I received no phone call; I would not be attending the New Year's service.

Then, on January 1st, God told me to write about my *season of waiting*, and what had surfaced in my life over the last three months. When I heard this instruction, I knew my return to church would not happen until I wrote about the current season in which I was living. I tried to finish writing it by mid-January, but God's timing is perfect, and I trusted Him.

In early January, the pastor prayed this prayer during one of the services: "I ask that what you are asking for comes to pass within the next four weeks. I don't know why I just prayed that." I knew why. I had been asking to return, and four weeks hence would have been mid-February. I finished writing the chapters I intended to write by then, but God had me write an additional chapter about the process I had just experienced. I didn't return to the church in February, either.

As the waiting came to a close, I received this scripture:

And he swore by Him who lives for ever and ever, who created the heavens and all that is in them, the earth and all that is in it, and the sea and all that is in it, and said, "There will be no more delay! But in the days when the seventh angel is about to sound his trumpet, the mystery of God will be accomplished, just as he announced to his servants the prophets."
Revelation 10:6-7 (NIV)

Knowing God speaks His word before it comes to pass, I found myself still waiting, but now I knew the end was drawing near: *"There will be no more delay."* God always confirms His Word, and in January, I received this written prophetic word from a prophetic listserve to which I subscribe. It confirmed what I already knew:

Listen to Me. I know what you have been through. I know the harshness of the past season that you have had to endure. I know the reality of that, but please understand that it was for your benefit; the benefit of strength; the benefit of your trust in Me. Those things that you have endured and gone through have made you stronger, if you believe they have. And, as you come out into a new season, you will find the strength that I have given to you will become a reality. It stretched you and caused you to walk with greater dignity, greater revelation, and greater focus than ever before. This new reality will benefit you in the season that is now unfolding before you. So leave those things in My hand. The things you endured will now become your ornaments – they tell the world, tell the enemy, you have been through something, and you have come out victoriously on this side of it. "This day, see yourself as victorious," says the Lord.

"The Trumpet" by Bill Burns, Faith Tabernacle

Though the process of healing lasted until mid- March, my s*eason of waiting* didn't end until the end of March. During the *season*, prophetic words were spoken or written that pertained to me, including the one mentioned above. But the word that had the most impact on me personally was spoken by the California pastor during her online service one Saturday in early February. At the prompting of the Lord, I watched the service online a few days later.

The pastor began the first segment of the service with a prophetic word of blessing. Then she began to speak prophetic words over individuals. When she came upon one woman, God's presence came over me and I knew the word she was speaking was for me too. I have never experienced His presence when a word was spoken over someone else, but I knew God was speaking directly to me, and I received his word. This season in which I had spent the past five months was coming to a close. The prophetic word was:

The Lord says, "You're pregnant, ready to give birth. You're holding your stomach because you are pregnant with destiny. You're carrying the seed. The glory of the Lord is going to be released in unlimited measures to God's people."

Then she said something about favor, but I couldn't understand it.

My *season of waiting* was coming to a close; a new season and fresh oil were upon me. It would take another six weeks before the season would conclude, but what transpired in those subsequent weeks was all part of God preparing me for my calling.

CHAPTER 24
Symbolic Gestures

There is nothing like encountering a trial to bring a person closer to their Lord and Savior, Jesus. I was no exception. As I began to seek God's face for understanding about what had happened between the pastor and me with regards to the draft book, I read 2 Chronicles, Chapter 29. This chapter refers to the time when King Hezekiah opened up and repaired the house of the Lord and realized it needed to be consecrated and cleansed, so he called the Levites into action. As I read this chapter, I decided to follow the same instructions as a *symbolic gesture*. What happened to me in those first sixteen days of consecration was incredible. Loosely following the guidelines, I began to pray for myself for the first eight days; then prayed for the church the next eight days, according to verse 17. We are holy temples unto God, and I decided to pull down strongholds and pray for restoration, as we both needed to be cleansed and healed.

As part of the consecration process, I prayed and walked around the pool of the community where I live. Having prayed for myself first, I asked for understanding and revelation of the purpose of the season. For me, it turned out to be a season of healing, and every time I thought the process was finished, more healing took place.

When praying for the church leadership and congregation, I asked that the walls of rejection, rebellion, pride, control, gossip, slander, deception, and anger that existed in the church be pulled down. One must understand, I am not pointing fingers, as every church and its people sin and fall short of the glory of God, as Romans 3:23 makes clear:

> *for all have sinned and fall short of the glory of God,* (NIV)

The purpose was to stop the enemy's efforts to steal from the church and myself God's plan and purpose for the congregation, my husband, and my destiny. All for His glory.

2 Chronicles 29:36 was the outcome of King Hezekiah's consecration:

> *Then Hezekiah and all the people rejoiced over what God had prepared for the people, because the thing came about suddenly.*

I wanted my *suddenly*. I wasn't about to let the enemy take away my blessing. Looking back on a conversation I had with two other people about marriage, the man stated, "One day, Julie's next husband is going to come and sweep her off feet," as if to say, it would happen *suddenly*. I believe this is exactly how he will come to me.

When the pastor had his personal breakthrough, he preached from Joshua 6. I mentioned this book and chapter earlier, but now I wasn't pulling down the strongholds. This time I was reading about Rahab, the prostitute, and how she hid spies in her home (Joshua, Chapter 2). She and her family were saved because of her action (Joshua 6:22-26). When the pastor preached on this, he said, simply, "Rahab submitted to authority." It was as if he were saying to me, "Everything will be OK." Not only had I been obedient to God's instruction, but I also submitted to the pastor's authority when he suggested I attend another church and I told him I would honor his request.

According to Joshua 2:21, Rahab and the two spies decided she would tie a scarlet cord in the window to ensure her safety:

> *"Agreed," she replied. "Let it be as you say." So she sent them away, and they departed. And she tied the scarlet cord in the window.* (NIV)

In Joshua 6:22, after the walls came down:

Joshua said to the two men who had spied out the land, "Go into the harlot's house and bring the woman and all she has out of there, as you have sworn to her."

As symbolic gesture, I tied a red ribbon in my bedroom window, so when it was time for me to return to the church, the pastor would symbolically know which house was mine.

The ribbon hung in my window and I waited for my *suddenly*. A word came suddenly at the end of March, but was not what I had hoped. It turned out to be the beginning of a new adventure and direction in my life. About a week after the door closed at church, I removed the red ribbon.

The Bible tells us in Joshua 6:25 that Rahab and her family lived in the midst of Israel. I believe *living in the midst* means that since she did God's will by following His instructions (Joshua 2:18), she lived in God's will and favor. Rahab's and her family's new position was a promotion from God. They lived in the midst; I now *dwell in the midst*.

I continue to walk around the pool, the kitchen island in my house, and even around the chairs of church at Friday night prayer meetings as a symbolic gesture to pull down strongholds in people's lives, as well as the strongholds that try to work against the church. It's not the action of walking around an area seven times that answers the prayer; it is the prayer itself that God answers. He knows my heart when I pray, and Yahweh answers my prayers according to His perfect will.

Taking communion is a symbolic gesture, as well, but for me, it is a reality, not a representation.

And when He had taken some bread and given thanks, He broke it and gave it to them, saying, "This is My body which is given for you; do this in remembrance of Me." And In the same way He took the cup after they had eaten, saying, "This cup

which is poured out for you is the new covenant in My blood.
Luke 22:19-20

Reading the words Jesus spoke, He did not say the bread or the wine represented his body and blood. He said the body and cup *are* given or poured out, as in the *now*. Partaking in communion is personal, not a ritual or tradition. I don't always partake, but when I do, it is meaningful and it is never the same prayer twice.

Symbolic gestures are just that, gestures. They are not used as ritualistic signs to create an atmosphere for the prayer to be heard; they are ways to acknowledge God as He moves in my life. I never want to put God in a box, as He is omniscient, omnipresent and omnipotent. I want to be open to how He wants to instruct and use me, and if that includes symbolism as a means to accomplish His purpose, then I am willing.

CHAPTER 25

Enjoy This Time with Your Son

As I made my bed one morning in January, the Lord spoke to me and said, "Enjoy this time with your son." I knew God was telling me, your husband is coming, so spend quality time with your son now. I thought my husband was coming soon, but God is Omniscient and He knows what is going to happen and when. God used this time to refine me so that I could be an example to my son.

Mac had been living with me since August of the previous year, when, after two years of being out of the house, he decided he would return home to save money. His first time away from home, Mac lived in the dorm at the university as a freshman and the following year in an apartment with a roommate. I had to acclimate myself to living with someone again: his idiosyncrasies, schedules, likes, and dislikes. We soon settled into a routine and enjoyed each other's company. For me, it was a time of preparation. I knew once God released him from the house, new things were in store for me.

I raised my son very differently than most Christians, and I believe he is the young man he is today because of it. I never attended church while I was married and raising Mac and my stepson. I did, however, pray, praise, and speak the Word of God into Mac's life and into the lives of my ex-husband and stepson, as well. In fact, I often quoted scriptures as a frame of reference for specific situations that presented themselves.

I believed and *stood* on God's promises for my son's life. The following scriptures are examples of God's promises:

> *For the word of God is living and active. Sharper than any double-edged sword, it penetrates even to dividing soul and spirit, joints and marrow; it judges the thoughts and attitudes of the heart.* Hebrews 4:12 (NIV)

> *And, so shall My word be that goes forth from My mouth; It shall not return to Me void, But it shall accomplish what I please, and it shall prosper in the thing for which I sent it.* Isaiah 55:11 (NKJV)

All the words spoken to my son – words of wisdom, encouragement, discipline, and love – have not returned void, as Isaiah 55:11 states. I cannot judge his relationship with Jesus; only he knows that. But I believe the day is coming when he will walk a dedicated life with Jesus as his Lord and Savior. In fact, as I prayed one night, I saw Mac shadowing the pastor as a preacher. About three weeks later, when Mac attended the Mother's Day church service at my request, I introduced him to a few people. One was a woman who, upon meeting him, proclaimed, "I see a preacher." It was a confirmation to me, but it threw Mac for a loop.

Mac is older now and has a better understanding of the Word of God. As he continues to learn life lessons, each lesson can be confirmed by a scripture. Two of the most profound lessons he learned while living with me dealt with money. The first experience occurred because he was trying to sell something because he wanted money immediately. He sold the item for very little money and said to me one day, "Mom, I should have waited to sell it. I got greedy and sold it for less than it was worth." Not many young adults learn a lesson about greed so early in life. I talked to him about it and was able to share:

> *For the love of money is a root of all sorts of evil, and some by longing for it have wandered away from the faith and pierced themselves with many griefs.* 1 Timothy 6:10

The other lesson he learned came about from an obedient action of mine. I drove myself to the train station and parked in the lot. Mac had left some money in the car console, so to prevent anyone from being tempted by it to break into the car, I picked up the money and put it in my purse. Often, I pray while I am on the train and I keep my eyes closed. As I prayed, I opened my eyes, and a woman with a blanket was sitting next to me quietly talking to the person next to her. I received an instruction to give the woman next to me some money. He showed me that I was to give her all but one dollar of Mac's money. I went into my purse, pulled out *all* the money, and handed it to her.

That evening, I told my son I had given the money he left in the car to a homeless couple. He said to me, "I thought I had less money in my wallet. Well, if the money wasn't important enough for to me to pick it up, then I guess I didn't need it." I told him the couple had thanked me profusely for the money and told me I didn't know how much they needed it.

I said to both my son and to them, "I don't, but God does."

Then my son and I discussed how they might use the money. Were they going to buy drugs or use it for necessities? I shared that what they did with the money was not for us to be concerned about; I had been obedient to the instruction. I prayed that they would use it for the purpose which God had intended. This time I shared:

> *Be anxious for nothing, but in everything by prayer and supplication with thanksgiving let your requests be made known to God.* Philippians 4:6

God will meet all of Mac's needs, as well as mine.

God has given me prophetic words to speak into my son's life. A recent word came as we walked to the train platform after parking the car one morning. God said, "Tell Mac to *keep learning.*" God wanted him to know that book learning was just as important as experiential learning. I gave my son the message, and he received it. We talked about the two types of learning, and how God was going to use Mac's sense of curiosity and desire for knowledge for His glory. I don't know if Mac fully understood the message, but I know the day will come when he will look back on that conversation and have a revelation.

Another word I spoke to Mac occurred when he first started attending the university. He is a biochemistry major, and before he ever started college, he told me he wanted to find a cure or treatment for a disease. I knew it was a God-given desire, as God gives us desires. So when they come to pass, He gets the glory. The word came to me a few days before I shared it with him. One day Mac came into my office excited about something he had learned in chemistry class. He shared the new information with me. I looked at him and said, "God is going to give you a calculation in the middle of the night. Write it down, as it is the key to unlocking the mystery of the disease." He received the word. Fast forward to Mother's Day. Mac came to church with me again, at my request.

> HONOR YOUR FATHER AND MOTHER (which is the first commandment with a promise), SO THAT IT MAY GO WELL WITH YOU, AND THAT YOU MAY LIVE LONG ON THE EARTH. Ephesians 6:2-3

During the message, the pastor said, "Often times God gives us a desire to accomplish something, but it isn't until years later when the desire comes to pass." I leaned over to my son and said, "The calculation." He nodded yes. I know God is preparing Mac for something, and the time we spend together is all part of His plan for both of us and our respective destinies.

He has watched me and witnessed firsthand my personal relationship with Jesus; that is the best teaching experience I can give my son. So we spend time together while we are both in the living room – me reading the Word, watching Christian television, or writing while Mac plays online video games or studies. When he is out of the house, I use the time to pray fervently, just me and the Holy Spirit. When he arrives home, I am usually praying; he doesn't say too much. Every day, we talk about various topics: I share something that happened during the day or evening and Mac shares what he learned in class or by reading online magazines such as *Time* or *Forbes*. He is a sponge for knowledge, and I have learned so much from him.

One talk in particular, just made me laugh. Mac asked, "Mom, do you know what Cryo Electron Microscopy (Cryo EM) is?"

I asked in response, "Does it have to do with freezing dead people?"

"Well," Mac said, "Cryo has to do with freezing." He then proceeded to explain the process of freezing water in liquid nitrogen. Then, he began explaining Cryo EM.

Throughout the conversation, I couldn't stop laughing. Mac naturally wondered if maybe I was laughing at him. I wasn't. I was laughing hysterically because, of all the questions my son has asked me about science, I have only known the answers to perhaps two of them. I explained to him that I usually don't know the answer to the science he is about to explain and found it funny how he continues to ask me about my knowledge of it, even though he already knows the answer, more than likely, is no. I have learned some very interesting facts over the time he has lived at the house and will miss him the day he moves out.

It was a Tuesday night, and I was watching the church service on my laptop, while my son sat at his computer playing a game. Mac could see the live stream as he played. At one point, the pastor stated, "The miracle is getting close to manifesting itself."

I screamed, "Yes, yes, yes!" I turned to my son and I explained that I would be returning to church soon. This opened the door for me to explain why I hadn't been attending church, which led to me talking about how his dad had treated me. He listened.

Finally, Mac told me that he didn't remember much about his childhood, but he did remember the day his dad had said the dreadful words, "I'm going to rip your face apart."

I explained that his comment, "That was scary, Mom. I thought you were going to get a divorce," was the catalyst for me to file for divorce.

I don't say too much to Mac about his dad, as it is his father. He is older now and he understands his father a bit better, but he seldom talks about his dad unless asked. When his former student teacher asked Mac if he had seen his father and how was he doing, Mac said briefly, "I saw him over Christmas vacation, and he has health issues."

After a year of living with me, God opened the door for Mac to move out. There is great favor on my son, and only God could have provided him a fully furnished one bedroom condominium on the fifteenth floor of a high rise in Central Phoenix to sublet. He had been wanting to move out of the house shortly after he arrived, but he waited and was blessed for waiting for God to move on his behalf. My son has first-hand experience of how God operates in his life and is walking into his own destiny, whether he believes it or not.

I cherished this time with Mac. When I shared with him the words God had spoken to me about enjoying my time with him, he just listened. I assured him that God would not only provide for me, but He would also provide for him. Mac was provided for; now it is my turn. I didn't know how long it would be, but I knew I was closer to my destiny. My son was out of the house, and a new season was upon me.

CHAPTER 26

Healing - Stay in the Process

Come, let us return to the LORD. He has torn us to pieces but he will heal us; he has injured us but he will bind up our wounds. After two days he will revive us; on the third day he will restore us, that we may live in his presence. Let us acknowledge the LORD; let us press on to acknowledge him. As surely as the sun rises, he will appear; he will come to us like the winter rains, like the spring rains that water the earth.
Hosea 6:1-3 (NIV)

God is the God of healing and restoration. The healing that took place over the six months while I was between ministries was incredible, yet every time I thought I was finished with the process, I discovered there was more healing to take place. What God starts, He will finish. He does everything perfectly and in His time.

... [He] is the Author and Perfecter of our faith ...
Hebrews 12:2 (NIV)

... the Alpha and the Omega, the Beginning and the End ...
Revelation 21:6 (NIV)

God completed the healing He had begun. It wasn't until mid-February that I truly understood the entire process. Each person or group of people represented an area of my life: the twelve years of my marriage, or the nine years since the divorce.

The first person I told about my marriage was a girlfriend I have known since 1981 when I lived in Tucson and worked at the university. We were both dating Englishmen at the time. She married hers, while I caught mine in bed with another woman. She also happened to call the same night I received the call from the pastor's cousin. We talked before and after the call from the church. She was so supportive, and the email she sent me the next day meant a lot to me. She wrote:

> *This break you are taking from the church is a much needed one, I think? Your eyes will be opened to something new coming into your life. ... It's all going to be good, Julie. You'll see!*

I held onto her words, "It's all going to be good, Julie. You'll see!" They reminded me of Romans 8:28:

> And we know that in all things God works for the good of those who love him, who have been called according to his purpose. (NIV)

The same day, the church posted a blog titled, *Stay in the Process.* I knew it was a word for me and I listened, though I didn't have full understanding of *the process* until I was actually in it for a while. At first, I thought I was out of the process because I told the pastor I would honor his request, but as time passed and God brought people into my path to share my marriage experience, I realized I was *in the process.*

The process began by the end of October with a few people at work. They knew I attended church regularly and love the Lord, as I would share how God moved in my life or through a word spoken from the pulpit. So when they asked what was going on at church, I began to tell each woman individually what had happened. They knew I was divorced, but I'd never shared the story behind my divorce. The women, most of whom are believers, heard the testimony of my marriage to my ex-husband for the first time, when I shared what happened at church, as the two stories were intertwined. They were all shocked. I had seen no reason to share details of my past marriage, as I felt it was important to keep moving forward, but God had other plans.

All of them were so supportive and couldn't believe what I had endured. Most of them commented on how long I had stayed in the marriage and asked why. I always responded, "For my son."

They would then say, "You have a lot of inner strength."

While I was sharing my testimony to my colleagues, a long-time girlfriend who'd known me when I was married but had never met my husband called. She knew some of what I had endured, but not the extent to which I began to share. Of course, many tears were shed in the telling. She said it best, "Since you have allowed God to heal you, with regard to men, He can now bring your husband to you." As she spoke, she acknowledged that many people are unwilling to relive the hurt from the past; but to move forward, sometimes the wound has to be reopened so it can heal properly.

Next, the Lord brought a family friend to me in early November. He had been my son's kindergarten student teacher and was like a son to my husband and me. Until the divorce, he came over for dinner regularly, and the doctor would always slip him some cash, as he was a university basketball player living on a stipend and scholarship. The basketball player had been on my heart long before I actually contacted him, but it wasn't until his email address popped up as I searched for a friend's address that I emailed him just to check in.

It was a divine appointment, and the healing God accomplished in that forty-five minute conversation was incredible. I don't remember how we got onto the subject of my marriage, but I do remember saying, "You saw how the doctor treated me."

He quietly said, "Yes." It was as though he was experiencing my pain by acknowledging what he had seen and heard. We talked a while longer, but it wasn't until three months later when I saw him in person that I was able to share that he represented all the family friends in my healing process. Mac was with me, and he just listened as we talked. During that conversation, he heard some things about his dad for the first time.

My sister-in-law called me one Sunday afternoon in mid-November and I again shared what had happened at church. She had met the pastor when she and my brother came to Phoenix to help paint my bedroom the prior December. Since she was one of the people who tried to dissuade me from marrying my husband, she was all too aware of how I was treated; nevertheless, she was shocked to hear the comments the pastor had made. We talked a long time about my ex and how the spirit of rejection manifested itself toward me. It was beginning to become easier to talk about my past marriage, but tears were still shed with each conversation. My sister-in-law represented my siblings: my brother and sister, both of whom are younger than I.

My stepson called me with a question one afternoon. It was an ordained moment, and as we talked, my stepson shared that he had a spirit of rejection on him. The problem that had afflicted his father was a generational curse, but I'd had no idea. I began to pray with him, and he was so remorseful about how his father had treated me. I explained to him that I had repeatedly forgiven his dad throughout the marriage; it was my faith that allowed me to stay longer than I should have.

After the conversation with my stepson, I thought I was through with the healing process. However, God had other plans, and in December, He opened the door for my mom and me to talk. This conversation dealt with my dad, and I started to cry as I shared what I had experienced at the voice and hand of my father. My mom had no idea of the harm my dad's critical spirit had caused me. She felt bad because she hadn't protected any of her children from his words. I explained to her that dad was only saying what he thought would help us be the best kids and later on become the best adults we could be. We both acknowledged the spirit of criticism passed down to my dad from his mom, my paternal grandmother.

I look back now, and even twenty minutes before he passed, he was criticizing me for the way I handled a conversation between him and his sister. I loved him right where he was in his character and understood him and his thought processes. And, more importantly, I forgave him, as I did the other men in my life, including the pastor.

After the conversation with my mom, I was sure the process must now be over. It was the end of the year, and now that my mom and I had talked, there was no one else in whom to confide the hurts. WRONG! About three weeks later, God opened the door for my son and I to talk again.

It was difficult trying to explain to Mac why I wasn't going to church anymore. What was I going to say? That during a phone call, the pastor had alluded that the leadership wanted to place a restraining order against me? It wouldn't speak well to any believer or unbeliever that the pastor of the church would make such a comment without seeking God's face or counseling me regarding any concerns he might have about my actions, so I withheld the whole story from Mac until mid-February. When I finally told him the truth, my son had nothing nice to say about the pastor or Christianity.

I explained to him that, as it says in Romans 3:23, we have all sinned and fallen short of the glory of God. Not one of us is perfect, and because we are not perfect, forgiveness needs to take place. I had forgiven the pastor; now Mac needed to do the same. My son said to me, "Mom, I don't care who your husband is. I just want you to be happy." One thing I know: God will not give me a husband who isn't perfect for me. I chose the first husband; now I would let God choose the one He had set aside for me from the beginning of time. I waited and trusted God, knowing that whoever the man was, my son and he would get along and respect each other. They would both have my best interest at heart, just as God does.

That ten-minute conversation produced a lot of tears on my behalf, and I thought, "Surely, now I have completed the healing process." But it wasn't yet complete. Over lunch one day with my immediate coworkers, the three women were talking about their bad experiences with their fathers. One of the women turned to me and said, "Looks like you are the only one who doesn't have father issues."

I huffed a laugh and said, "No. Let me tell you what I experienced. If I start to cry, bear with me, as I am still healing. I have shed so many tears that had I collected them, I'd have had enough to fill the Grand Canyon. I am writing a book in which I discuss what I experienced." And I began to share. That was the end of January.

A few weeks later, God opened the door for me to talk with the woman who attends the church and had reached out to me over the six months of my absence. While I was away, she had faithfully checked in on me and invited me to join her at various conventions that featured well-known preachers and teachers. In February, I was led to take her out for dinner, and God's presence permeated my car as we shared. God was confirming and moving between the two of us. She said she wanted to give me a DVD about Karla Faye Tucker, called *Forevermore*. That was a Thursday. On Saturday, I watched the movie, as my son was out of the house.

As I watched, God began to stir within me and the tears again started flowing. The movie reminded me of various things, like how much I love the Lord and I would do anything He asked of me and how people had supported me through the six-month ordeal. Importantly, the movie had a conclusion. Perhaps the most profound scene for me was when Karla Faye prayed and released her husband back into God's hands. I had done that with the pastor. Whether he would be my husband or not, he was in God's hands, and I could only pray for God's will for both of us.

After getting myself together, I called the woman who'd given me the DVD, who I now consider a friend. I tried to talk, but couldn't. I was released to share with her the reason I wasn't attending the church. After a few moments, I regained my composure and shared what the pastor had said and my reaction to his words. My friend was shocked, but said, "Now I understand why you are waiting for your release to return. I couldn't figure out why you were waiting if you were healed."

But I wasn't completely healed yet. Though I remembered everything, I had suppressed the emotions and hurts. I had a son to care for and needed to be strong for him. As I talked with my friend, God revealed to me the healing process He was working in me and brought to mind all the people He had brought into my path and how each person had some knowledge of how my ex-husband had treated me. Toward the end of the conversation, I had the revelation that an upcoming lunch meeting with my former staffer would be the conclusion of my healing process.

As a staffer, she had experienced my marriage in a completely different way. I remembered from a chain of emails she sent that the reason she'd moved to another city was because she was afraid of workplace violence, even going so far as to ask if I was in denial. I explained to her that I was not in denial, and I would explain everything when we met for lunch in mid-February.

En route to lunch in Payson, a small town about ninety miles northeast of Phoenix, I listened to Christian music, enjoyed God's glory in the mountains, and prayed that God would direct the conversation. We met at 11 a.m. and talked for three hours. I hadn't seen my friend since she had visited Phoenix a year ago in February to attend a three-day convention. What God did in a three-hour conversation was the final touch in my healing process, because this conversation also included all the hurts caused by my dad. My friend couldn't believe what she was hearing.

Then she shared how she had been afraid for her life and mine. I knew my ex had tried to kick the office door down because I had seen his footprint on the door. However, I hadn't known that she was in the office when this happened. I was in shock. I had never lived in fear, as he had never been physically abusive.

As I drove back to Phoenix, God spoke: "You are ready." I began to cry, because I knew it. The healing process was complete. My friend from church had spoken over me a few days before my lunch in Payson and said, "Yes, the healing is complete." She told me she'd gotten goose bumps when she said it, which was my confirmation.

The healing came full circle when I received a series of texts from my ex-husband telling me he was sorry for his actions toward me. *I didn't realize what the drugs were doing to me and you at the time. I still love you.* But it wasn't until the text that stated, *Please forgive me,* that I said to my son, "I need to respond to this text."

I wrote back, *I forgive you. I loved you when we were married. Now I move forward.*

He tried calling and sending another text about getting back together, but I did not respond to either. The last text he sent me that evening said, *You are not a Christian. You are a liar.* His comment reaffirmed that I had made the right decision to divorce him.

I am healed of the past hurts. It was a process that was uncomfortable at first, but became easier as time passed and I continued to share my testimony. Although I tried to suppress what I had experienced from my ex-husband, I had to admit that those twelve years are part of who I am today. This testimony could help someone else reach their destiny by explaining the process God used to help me reach mine, with or without the pastor as my husband. I stayed in the process and, at times it was painful; but the joy I have now is invaluable as I see the big picture unfold in front of me. As Jeremiah 29:11 says:

> *For I know the plans I have for you," declares the LORD, "plans to prosper you and not to harm you, plans to give you hope and a future.* (NIV)

CHAPTER 27
Personal Victories

Throughout my *season of waiting,* I grew spiritually and had many personal victories. Little did I know what God was preparing me for; it was bigger than I could have imagined – more than being a pastor's wife. God will never send us out before we are ready, and there were still areas in my life that needed to be transformed. Although I didn't realize it at the time, that is why God kept the pastor and me apart. He had to perform some character surgery on me.

Two weeks after my last conversation with the pastor, I was prompted to watch the California pastor online. She commented that she would be traveling to Phoenix to be a guest speaker. I looked up the church where I knew she spoke occasionally, and sure enough, she would be there the next day, Sunday. My visit to this new church was the first time I attended another church during my season of separation, preparation, and healing. It was an anointed service, and at the end of the praise and worship portion, God spoke to me: "The walls are coming down."

Then she spoke the same words God had just spoken to me, which was further confirmed by the man of God, the senior pastor of the church. I immediately thought of my pastor's walls – anger and rejection – the walls I had been praying to come down, but I had no idea that the word applied to me, as well. This victory and realization came almost a year later.

> 'The latter glory of this house will be greater than the former,' says the LORD of hosts, 'and in this place I will give peace,'

declares the LORD of hosts." Haggai 2:9

Considering everything that happened at church and work over the last two years, in the natural, I should have been anxious, but I wasn't. The worse the situations became in the natural, the stronger I became in the spiritual. I walked in a peace I couldn't explain. As Philippians 4:7 says:

> *and the peace of God, which surpasses all understanding, will guard your hearts and minds through Christ Jesus.* (NKJV)

I had a new peace, but it was even **deeper** than peace.

I didn't understand it at first, but as I began to meditate on what I was experiencing, I received Hebrews 12:27-28:

> *This expression, "Yet once more," denotes the removing of those things which can be shaken, as of created things, so that those things which cannot be shaken may remain. Therefore, since we receive a kingdom which cannot be shaken, let us show gratitude, by which we may offer to God an acceptable service with reverence and awe;*

That scripture explained exactly what I was experiencing. I could not be moved by the circumstances that were in front of me. God's Kingdom cannot be shaken, and neither could I. *On Earth as It Is in Heaven.* As time passed, I understood that whatever might try to come against me in the future would not stand. I was *unshakable*.

One day at work, a professor entered into my office and asked how I was doing, knowing I had a very last-minute deadline to meet. It was stressful, but I persevered. When I answered, "Unshakable," he appeared startled.

"That was not the word I was expecting," he explained. He then looked up at my white board to see which scriptures and words I had written on it. I believe he knew I was drawing my strength from God.

Although it took six months, the healing from the hurt caused by my ex-husband was my biggest victory! It was a process I needed to go through before my next marriage could be successful – I needed to be healed. Months had passed and I now found myself having to deal with bitterness toward the pastor. I had never experienced bitterness before, but for whatever reason, I recognized that although I was praying for the pastor and the church, I was hurt. I shared my feelings with a couple of friends, openly confessing my bitterness to them. I prayed, opened the Word, and received James 5:16:

> *Therefore confess your sins to each other and pray for each other so that you may be healed. The prayer of a righteous man is powerful and effective.* (NIV)

Talk about confirmation!

I woke up the next morning and told the Lord I was going to put on my spiritual sackcloth and repent for the bitterness and hurt in me. Praise the Lord, He is faithful and my friends really encouraged me that morning. First I received a text from a woman whose heart is genuine. The text had a scripture verse and the following message: *The healing will happen quicker than you think.* I took the day off work and was home alone. I had already planned to clean the house before I recognized the bitterness. As I cleaned, a spiritual cleansing of my heart took place at the same time. I praised the Lord, listened to music, and prayed. By late afternoon, I realized that God had healed me of the pain and forgiveness had taken place. Quick and painless! Praise the Lord.

Later in the evening, a friend who attends the church told me the church services would be broadcast internationally. God was testing my heart. I could genuinely tell her I was happy for the church and the pastor. The test happened quickly, and the best part: I PASSED!

As I continued to follow God's instructions, read the Word of God, and interpret visions and dreams, I found myself walking a new path. It was a path of living in the Spirit, but it was happening in the natural. I didn't understand what I was experiencing until I heard the term *spiritual reality*. That was it! I was living heaven on earth, just like the spiritual dating and being sensitive to God around me.

The best example of *spiritual reality* happened one day when I was getting ready to exit the train at work. God said, "Go the other way."

I thought, "Go the other way?" I had never walked to my office from the other direction, as it was not a major thoroughfare. I thought to myself, "OK. I will determine how long it takes me to walk to the office going the other direction," trying to rationalize the reason I was walking a different path. I was thinking in the natural. God showed me what He was doing with the instruction via a prophetic listserve to which I subscribe. When I opened up the email, I read the following:

> *Pay attention to the signs around you, for truly I will speak to you in a variety of ways and will show you things that you need to see in the natural realm so that you can understand what I am doing in the spiritual realm. At this time you can make your plans, but you must hold them loosely as with an open hand so that you can be led by the Spirit. Your next step, My guidance, and even your safety depends on your ability to follow, says the Lord. Proverbs 16:9 "A man's heart plans his way, but the Lord directs his steps."*
> "Small Straws in a Soft Wind," by Marsha Burns, Faith Tabernacle

I wrote the following in my daily journal:

> *Today's Small Straws was profound, as I walked a different direction into work at the Lord's leading. As I write, it is significant and represents what God is doing. I am on a different path, direction than what I thought. I need to be open to what He is doing and watch for the signs in the natural and in the spiritual. This is PROFOUND! What a revelation.*

As I continued toward my destiny, this natural path led to a deeper understanding of what God was doing in my life. He told me to take a different path. What I thought God had in store for me was not what I expected. I had to hold the plans and ideas loosely. As I waited for the Lord to open the door, some options lay before me. Knocking on all the doors that presented themselves to me, I trusted God to open the right one. The doors included a new job, retiring, the book I was writing, a husband, ministry, or any combination of the five.

Understanding that God holds the key to my life allowed me to be open to His leading. Not knowing which, when, and how any of these possibilities would come to pass, I was in a place of complete dependency on Him. In my twenty-nine year walk with the Lord, I have never had to be so trusting of Yahweh, rather than my own ideas. I knew I was living the verse John 3:30:

> "He must increase, but I must decrease."

It was a personal victory, and now He could begin to use me for His glory.

My personal victories were overcoming experiences. To overcome can be described as prevailing over triumphing over something. I overcame hurts and the desire to control my destiny. As I continued to grow, God took me from one level to the next. Growth is a continual process and, if allowed, it will bring us into victories and ultimately the destiny to which we are called.

> For whatever is born of God overcomes the world; and this is the victory that has overcome the world – our faith. 1 John 5:4

CHAPTER 28

It Was a Test

Early New Year's morning, God spoke to me on six different occasions. This is what He said:
- "I'm getting ready to do something new."
- "This is your year."
- "I will give you a place of rest."
- "There is a hedge around you. They can't get you. I will protect you."
- "End the book with a salvation call."
- "It was a test!"

I couldn't believe it – A TEST? I had no idea that all the instructions I had followed and everything I had endured over the past sixteen months was to test my heart toward Him. I was willing to do what He said, even when I knew the outcome might be unpleasant. He would take me to the next level. He brought to mind what He spoke to me in the summer prior to the New Year: "I will use you in a mighty and powerful way." The tests determined my destiny and how I would be utilized for His glory.

The Bible has many references to God testing His people; tests of the heart and mind toward Him, tests of obedience, tests of faith, and tests dealing with character. Each test had a specific purpose, and it wasn't until I went through my tests that I really understood the purpose of each one. Just as many people in the Bible were tested, I also encountered tests that were crucial to my walk with the Lord and destiny.

First, it is important to understand that a test from God is different than being tempted by the enemy. The old saying, "The devil made me do it," is actually incorrect. The devil tempts us, but we have free will to do, to choose, or not to do or partake in the word or action. *The Merriam-Webster Dictionary* defines the word tempt as "to entice to do wrong by promise of pleasure or gain."

> Let no one say when he is tempted, "I am being tempted by God"; for God cannot be tempted by evil, and He Himself does not tempt anyone. James 1:13

God is *holy,* perfect in goodness and righteousness, as defined by the *Merriam-Webster Dictionary*. He cannot *tempt* someone to do wrong, as He does no wrong. A test, according to the *Merriam-Webster Dictionary,* is defined as "a critical observation, examination, or evaluation; trial." How God would use me for His glory depended on my willingness to be obedient and follow His instructions, most of which had to do with the pastor.

Tests of the heart and mind were the difficulties I experienced during my walk, and they brought me closer to God. As Deuteronomy 8:2 says:

> "You shall remember all the way which the LORD your God has led you in the wilderness these forty years, that He might humble you, testing you, to know what was in your heart, whether you would keep His commandments or not.

Through all the various circumstances, God had been looking at my heart and mind toward Him. Did I get mad at Him? Was I upset with the trial in front of me? Did I murmur because of the situation? Was I going to gossip to anyone about what I was experiencing? The answer was no on all accounts. I very rarely ever spoke of the trials or tribulations. I would share snippets of what I was experiencing with friends, but never the full picture. I knew that most of them couldn't receive what I was saying, so it was better to keep my mouth shut. Instead, I pressed in to God by reading my Bible, praying, or lighting a candle as a votive offering, a symbolic gesture of my gratitude and devotion to the great I AM.

I believe God is continually testing my heart and mind, and the more I press in to know Him, the deeper the awareness. These are spiritual encounters that bring me to a place of humbleness, knowing that only by His grace do I live the prosperous life He has given me. Prosperity does not equal financial means, although it can have financial blessings attached to it; rather, it means to live Galatians 5:22-23:

> But the fruit of the Spirit is love, joy, peace, patience, kindness, goodness, faithfulness, gentleness, self-control; against such things there is no law.

Situations presented themselves and the way I handled them was directly related to the first two statements God spoke to me on January 1st. I thought they were related to the pastor being my husband, but it was something bigger.

God's tests of my obedience and faith are the reason this book exists and are discussed throughout the testimony. Obedience to God means to follow his laws, decrees, statutes, and commands, as they are mentioned in the New Testament. Many laws of the Old Testament were given by the Lord, only to show us that we are fallible and sinful, and it is only by grace that we have a relationship with Jesus.

Faith tests are those instructions from God to do something that is usually outside of our comfort zone. The best example of a faith test is found in the Old Testament, in Genesis, Chapter 22. God instructs Abraham to sacrifice his son, Isaac. I experienced several faith tests, including the instructions to give the pastor my spiritual résumé and various notes, not to mention the question, would I continue to believe the pastor was my husband? I stayed in the process. Besides testing my heart, mind, and the keeping of His commandments, God tested my faith and trust in Him. As with Abraham, my faith would be counted as righteousness.

The best example of trusting God in the Bible is the story of Shadrach, Meshach, and Abed-nego in Daniel, Chapter 3, all of whom served in the king's court, but refused to worship any other god but the one true God. They were literally thrown into a fiery furnace – and survived. They trusted Yahweh and survived the circumstance. My trials by furnace were intense and lasted a while; just when I thought they were over, the heat would grow even fiercer than it had been previously. These furnace tests are best described in Romans 5:3:

> And not only this, but we also exult in our tribulations, knowing that tribulation brings about perseverance;

Perseverance is further explained in 2 Peter 1:5-7:

> For this very reason, make every effort to add to your faith goodness; and to goodness, knowledge; and to knowledge, self-control; and to self-control, perseverance; and to perseverance, godliness; and to godliness, brotherly kindness; and to brotherly kindness, love. (NIV)

When Papa asked me how I was doing one evening, I responded by putting my arm up and circling it with my other hand, saying, "I'm staying in the eye of the storm, while I watch everything happen around me." I could see the spiritual battle. He smiled and walked away.

When the trials come – and they will – get into that place of peace and faith, trusting God to get you through the storm. Read the Psalms; written by King David, many of them deal with the attacks he experienced from his enemies. Psalm 18 deals with distress and is one of my favorites. Psalm 18:11 says:

> He made darkness His hiding place, His canopy around Him, Darkness of waters, thick clouds of the skies.

Sometimes God hides Himself in a dark cloud. Just like a forest fire produces a dark smoke, one can imagine that the burning bush blazed and created a dark smoke while God spoke to Moses about the deliverance of the Israelites, as is recounted in Exodus, Chapter 3. In 2 Chronicles 6:1, a dark cloud was also found in Solomon's temple, when the glory of the Lord filled the place:

Then Solomon said, "The LORD has said that He would dwell in a dark cloud."

Just as God showed up as a dark cloud in the Bible, He shows up in trials and tribulations, using these situations to bring us to a new place in Him. It could be a place of repentance, growth, or awareness. God knows what He wants to achieve in each of us; the pastor and I were no different. For me, the dark cloud of not attending church allowed me to experience a healing process; after this process was completed, the burden was lifted.

God tested me in the furnace and in the refining fire to ensure my character remained true to Him. The big tests lasted well over a year and turned into tests of refinement. Having passed both the big and refining tests at church and work, I was ready for the next door to open.

On a spiritual level, I understood that the closer I drew to my destiny, the stronger the attacks became, but the enemy was defeated at Calvary, and I stand on that promise. God can use everything that happens in our lives for His glory, and my tests were no exception. While being tested, I kept my eyes on the Lord, continually reading, praising, worshipping, and praying – never questioning, cursing, or becoming anxious. I trusted Him, knowing He knew the perfect time for everything to take place in my life. Tests will continue and they are for our benefit. Welcome them and embrace them, as God is using them to establish His character in you. I know any tests that I experience are for my personal growth, which means promotion will follow.

CHAPTER 29

Tears

A longtime friend once told me I had the gift of tears. At the time, I didn't have a full understanding of her comment, but the closer my relationship with Jesus becomes, the more I cry. Tears have significance to me: they represent joy, thanksgiving, healing, cleansing, growth, confirmation, and vindication.

> *Vindicate me, O LORD, for I have walked in my integrity, And I have trusted in the LORD without wavering.* Psalm 26:1

The God-given instructions I followed were all met with resistance by the pastor and sometimes the church leadership.

I understood that the leadership was looking out for the pastor, as he is the shepherd of the flock, but they didn't take the time to investigate my side of the story. It seemed as if they assumed that since Pastor was the senior pastor and they were in leadership, they were right and I was wrong. With each assignment, I was vindicated from the pulpit. I usually cried when I shared the situation with someone the first time; they were tears of vindication.

Tears of confirmation always come when I share what God is about to do in my life. When I speak something prophetic, I know God uses the tears as a way to confirm that my words are the truth. When God has spoken to or shown me something and I speak it for the first time publically, I usually cry. I never know when the tears will flow, but whenever they do, I know what I speak is true.

A particular incident comes to mind. I have been going to the same aesthetician for nine years and have told her many stories about how God has moved in my life. I was sharing with her how I would be able to retire from the university in April, and within five months I would know what God was going to do in my life, when I started to weep hysterically. That was in November. The answer came at the end of March, just as I had sensed in my spirit and told her, but what I thought He was going to do and what He did were two different things.

When God takes me to another level of spiritual growth, I cry. As a child, I experienced growing pains, as most children do. My bones and muscles were stretching, and my body often ached. That is what it is like to grow in the Lord. I ached as God stretched me through my personal walk with Him. As I grew, I learned lessons and experienced trials that were painful; it hurt, and I cried. Crying was a release for the pain, just like taking a warm bath was the solution for my body aches while growing as an adolescent. Growing pains are part of life, both spiritually and physically, and tears are a release from the pain.

Tears of cleansing are those shed following a painful experience and are used to cleanse oneself. I liken cleansing tears to rain. As a torrential rain washes away the dirt and dust that has accumulated on the streets, cars, or buildings, so do tears wash away past hurts and pains. The personal heartaches I experienced and have mentioned throughout the book and the cleansing tears that accompanied them allowed me to move forward.

> So let us know, let us press on to know the LORD. His going forth is as certain as the dawn; And He will come to us like the rain, Like the spring rain watering the earth. Hosea 6:3

I experienced incredible healing during my season *in between ministries*. It was also a time of preparation, and I shed not only cleansing tears, but tears of healing. The tears came because I was devastated that the church leadership saw me as a threat to the pastor's life. Having forgiven them, I still couldn't get over the fact that they perceived me in such a way. I told a friend that I needed to give the statement to God and stop thinking about it; otherwise I would not be able to move forward. She agreed. I know the enemy would have loved to keep me in a place of devastation, remembering the comment again and again, but as a co-heir with Christ, I am victorious. I cried for at least a month before I could finally release this burden to God, but it took almost a year before I was completely healed of the unfortunate incident.

but thanks be to God, who gives us the victory through our Lord Jesus Christ. 1 Corinthians 15:57

While struggling with comments and perceptions from the church leadership, I was also dealing with the hurts from my marriage. The tears came as God began to heal me. Until I began this journey, I was unaware that I had suppressed my ex-husband's comments and actions. As God began to bring to mind various incidents from the past, I would cry. The more I shared with family and friends about the way I was treated, the more I cried. The fortunate part about all the crying was the more I cried, the closer I drew to a complete healing. It wasn't until mid-February, that I obtained total victory over the past hurts.

When I meditate on God, the Creator, the Author and Finisher of my life, the Alpha and the Omega, the Potter (the list of attributes goes on), I am so thankful for all He has done, is doing, and is going to do in my life. Amazement at how awesome He is will occasionally bring unexpected tears of thanksgiving. When sharing a blessing with someone, I sometimes cry, thankful for ALL that He does in my life. To be in continual praise and thanksgiving is a wonderful place to exist.

Enter His gates with thanksgiving And His courts with praise. Give thanks to Him, bless His name. Psalm 100:4

And as Psalm 30:5 says:

> ... *Weeping may last for the night, But a shout of joy comes in the morning.*

Tears of joy often come when I am blessed in some way; often they are tears of thanksgiving. Following an instruction that leads to helping someone, recognizing that God has His hand on a situation, or just thanking Him for a glorious day will make tears well up in my eyes. Tears of joy are always welcome.

The closer my relationship to Jesus becomes, the more in awe I am of Him. This brings about tears of humility. Who am I to receive such grace? I don't think I can put into words how humbled I am by His greatness. I meditate on how He created the earth, the sun, the moon; how He knows the number of hairs on each of our heads; how He knows when we are happy, sad, and hurting; how He knows our sicknesses, our weaknesses, and our strengths.

Tears are an integral part of my walk with the Lord. I often find myself having to explain the tears when they show up unexpectedly while speaking with someone. When they come, I know their purpose and embrace them.

> *and He will wipe away every tear from their eyes; and there will no longer be any death; there will no longer be any mourning, or crying, or pain; the first things have passed away."*
> Revelation 21:4

CHAPTER 30

Trust God

God taught me many lessons over my twenty-nine years as a believer, but I experienced three major lessons during my *season of waiting* in which I had trusted Him in all situations: (1) the battle is God's, not mine; (2) sacrifice; and (3) don't react to the situation.

> *I will say to the LORD, "My refuge and my fortress, My God, in whom I trust!"* Psalm 91:2

Early in my walk with the Lord, I understood that any opposition I faced, whether at work or with family and friends, was usually a spiritual battle. I learned how to pray Ephesians 6:13-17, which states:

> *Therefore, take up the full armor of God, so that you will be able to resist in the evil day, and having done everything, to stand firm. Stand firm therefore, HAVING GIRDED YOUR LOINS WITH TRUTH, and HAVING PUT ON THE BREASTPLATE OF RIGHTEOUSNESS, and having shod YOUR FEET WITH THE PREPARATION OF THE GOSPEL OF PEACE; in addition to all, taking up the shield of faith with which you will be able to extinguish all the flaming arrows of the evil one. And take THE HELMET OF SALVATION, and the sword of the Spirit, which is the word of God.*

I recognized the battle wasn't against me, it was Christ in me.

Although I'd always been passionate about praying, especially for others, it wasn't until last year when I finally understood my calling as an intercessor. Facing the enemy head on comes naturally. I tell friends, "The enemy can't get to me; it's like I live in a bubble which protects me from the fiery darts of the evil one." One evening at church while praising the Lord, I received spoken confirmation of this statement. A man sitting behind me tapped my shoulder and said, "The devil is so afraid of you."

"I know," I acknowledged, and continued praising God during the corporate worship. People don't realize the authority God has given them to overcome all situations. His written Word and praise and worship are weapons He has given us to defeat the enemy. But sometimes, as a believer, you just have to stand and trust God.

While writing the letter to the church leadership, I prayed. Before hitting the SEND button, God said, "Open My Word." I did and was given 2 Chronicles 20:15, 17 and 20, which states:

> ... thus says the LORD to you, "Do not fear or be dismayed because of this great multitude, for the battle is not yours but God's.

> 'You need not fight in this battle; station yourselves, stand and see the salvation of the LORD on your behalf, O Judah and Jerusalem.' Do not fear or be dismayed; tomorrow go out to face them, for the Lord is with you."

> "... put your trust in the LORD your God and you will be established. Put your trust in His prophets and succeed."

Reading the scriptures, I knew there was nothing I could do, say, or pray to change the situation. I had to trust God and His promise: "You need not fight this battle; station yourself."

I lifted my voice to the Lord and said, "I will let you fight this one."

Of course, I continued to pray for the pastor and the leadership, but the fight was not mine. The enemy tried to close the door so I would miss my blessing and husband, but I trusted Him completely and in due season I returned to church.

Trusting God's word, *"the battle is not yours"* took on a new meaning a few days later. As I began to reflect on my marriage, God showed me how I'd always defended myself, throughout my life. First, I defended myself against my dad and his criticism, then against my ex-husband. My ex would tell me I was nothing or nobody, and I would respond, "Don't say that. I *am* somebody." I understood why my ex was putting me down: it made him feel better about himself, as he had a spirit of rejection and low self-esteem. Quite often, my self-defense would lead to a yelling match. Interestingly, I had never raised my voice to anyone before I was married, and I haven't done it again since my divorce.

As God brought to mind my self-defense mechanism and the yelling, all I could do was cry. It took some time, but I understood why I had been unable to respond to the pastor when he questioned me about the notes and the book. I couldn't defend myself. I was actually being led by the Spirit to keep my mouth shut. I had responses ready in my head but was never led to speak them.

It was as if I was a lamb headed to slaughter. There was nothing I could say to change the pastor's mind, so I kept quiet. As Matthew 27:12 says:

> And while He was being accused by the chief priests and elders, He did not answer.

When I read this scripture, I knew God would fight the battle for me. I had to trust His promises and know He was fighting on my behalf. Sometimes no response is the best response, so God can fulfill His plan.

There is a saying:

> If you love something, let it go.
> If it comes back to you, it's yours forever.

If it doesn't, then it was never meant to be.

– Unknown

Although I didn't understand it at the time, I sacrificed the pastor and church attendance, leading us both to progress to the respective places God intended for us. Just as Abraham offered Isaac as a sacrifice to the Lord, I was doing the same with the pastor and the church. I had never sacrificed anything to the Lord before this incident. God provided a ram as a replacement for Isaac; I now had to trust that God would bring my husband back to me because I was willing to give him up. About two months into my season of waiting, God spoke to me and said, "Because you were willing to give up the pastor, I will give him back to you." I waited in faith for God's word to come to pass. In due season, God brought us together at an event. Now it was up to the pastor to decide the next steps.

Many scriptures describe God's promises to His people. I received the following scriptures over time, as confirmation of His promise that the pastor was my husband. I believed and stood on them, but as the woman, I could only wait.

> *I know that You can do all things, And that no purpose of Yours can be thwarted.* Job 42:2

> *God is not a man, that He should lie, Nor a son of man, that He should repent; Has He said, and will He not do it? Or has He spoken, and will He not make it good?* Numbers 23:19

> *"For I the LORD will speak, and whatever word I speak will be performed. It will no longer be delayed, for in your days, O rebellious house, I will speak the word and perform it," declares the Lord GOD.* Ezekiel 12:25

Finally, I learned not to react. It is human nature to react when a situation is uncomfortable. Like the Israelites, the pastor was ready to throw stones at me, as I was the one God was using to take him to the next level, to the place called *there*. He reacted and called before asking God for direction on how to respond. This is a very hard lesson to learn, as the flesh wants to rise up quickly and respond without seeking God for the purpose or the answer to the situation.

I had to put the same lesson into action when I received my year-end donation receipt from the church. While I was *in between ministries,* I tithed using the online donation link on the church's website, expecting the tithes and offerings to be included on the receipt. They weren't. Immediately, I wanted to call the church office to ask why my gifts had not been noted. I had questions. Had they received the donations? Did the money go into a black hole? I reacted, thinking maybe this was a sign for me to call the church, rather than waiting for them to call me. I was upset, even though I had my receipts. I called a friend immediately, left a message, and asked her to pray; then I started to pray. I walked around the community pool and asked for guidance about whether I should call or leave it alone.

As I continued to pray, I heard, "It is a test." Then I realized that the devil would have liked nothing more than for me to step out of my wait and my destiny. I stopped, experienced peace, and left it alone. I did not make that call. Later on when I talked to my friend, she commented that she was glad I hadn't called and agreed that the enemy was eager to take me out of place.

The lesson: step back from the situation. Don't react. Trust God to reveal what needs to be done. He will provide the answer in His perfect timing; then act according to His answer. Would I react, or would I walk in peace? I walked in peace! I learned to step back, listen to what was being said, either verbally or in reading scripture, and take it to God before responding. As Proverbs 29:20 says:

> *Do you see a man who speaks in haste? There is more hope for a fool than for him.* (NIV)

I had never had to trust God to the extent I found myself now having to trust Him; from the instructions He gave me to the storms I endured to the *season of waiting*. In every situation, I trusted His Word, stood on it, and knew He would guide me in each situation, which ultimately would lead to my destiny. I was now beginning to walk in a place of complete trust in Him, letting my own flesh and natural thoughts go. And as I continued to trust God, doors began to open.

CHAPTER 31
My Setback Was a Setup

A pastor said it best in January: "How many had a tough 2013? Well, it was a setup for 2014." A few days earlier I had heard, *"Your setback is a setup"* while watching a young man give his testimony on a Christian television program. I understood exactly what the pastor was saying, as stepping away from the church for a season, while looking like a setback, was actually God setting me up for my next season.

In the natural, it didn't look good. I was not attending the church and had very little contact with anyone. But, I remained faithful to God with my prayers, praise, tithes and offerings, and my obedience. I trusted Him to fulfill the words spoken by various prophets. Prophetic words were spoken over me about my husband, ministry, and where it would take us – to the nations. As God's Word says in Lamentations 3:37:

> Who is there who speaks and it comes to pass, Unless the Lord has commanded it?

The words the pastor and I spoke during our final conversation happened because the Lord *commanded it*. But God gave me another interpretation of the same scripture. The *New Living Translation Bible* states:

> Can anything happen without the Lord's permission? (NLT)

I received this revelation when I was pondering the last conversation before I *honored his request* and spent a season away from the church. I asked myself, "Why did we say the things we said to each?" The answer is that the Lord allowed it to happen. God gave permission for exactly those words to be spoken. He knew we needed to be delivered and healed of issues, so we spoke the right words, enabling us to move toward our respective places.

I continued writing *in between ministries,* knowing I would return to church once I had recorded the events of the past six months. God even showed me what to wear on the day of my return, my best ensemble. And as much as I thought it was my vain imagination, I sensed that upon my return, an explosion would begin. It did, but not the one I was expecting. It was a setup for the next season.

A handshake, which is discussed in Chapter 32, *The Handshake – Betrayal to Promotion,* ushered me into a new season, took me to a new level in the Lord, and led me to a new church home the very next day, Sunday. Within twelve hours of one door closing, God opened the next door. Details about this are revealed in Chapter 33, *Suddenly.* Unbeknownst to me, I needed the setback for my own personal growth. Now, without a shadow of a doubt, I knew the pastor was not my husband. Although I'd had the faith to believe he was, he closed that door. And with the closing of that door, I was now on a different path to the same destiny. But now it was greater than I could imagine. God had told me, "It's big; be humble," a few years earlier and confirmed His word at the new church. All this time I had thought I was to be a pastor's wife and in charge of the women's ministry, but God had other plans in mind – although that could still be part of His plan.

The new church is small in attendance, compared to the one from which I was released. I had attended the new church twice during my *season of waiting,* both times because the California pastor was preaching. The first time I went on my own initiative, with the following scripture as my confirmation to go:

> Nathan replied to the king, "Whatever you have in mind, go

ahead and do it, for the LORD is with you." 2 Samuel 7:3 (NIV)

The second time was at the California pastor's invitation in late January to an event being held in March. The weekend was powerful. At the women's ministry meeting, she preached *The Kiss of Judas*. Little did I know, the message about Judas' betrayal of Jesus with a kiss before he went to the cross, died, and was resurrected, was prophetic and foreshadowed what was to come in my life in the very near future.

The new church was a miracle, my miracle waiting to happen. The very first Sunday I attended, the women's ministry leader remembered me from three weeks earlier. The smaller church allows for greater intimacy, and I quickly settled in. I was where God wanted me to be. Prayer meetings are held on Fridays, and having a fondness to pray, I attended. Almost immediately, I was asked to pray for others. As I prayed, I had words of knowledge for people and shared them accordingly. It was something I had wanted to do at the other church, but was rarely given the opportunity.

From the pulpit, the man of God asked my name and how I'd learned about the church. This led me to give a brief testimony about how God had prepared me in October to discover the church. This man of God knew more about me in five to seven minutes of conversation than the other pastor learned about me in my five years attending his church; except what he read in the draft book after I'd stepped away.

At week five, a prophet spoke a word to me, which put things in perspective regarding the ministry. He also told me that he had a radio program which broadcasts in seven markets on nine different stations in the South. At week six, I was interviewed for the radio show. It was a precursor of things to come. I was obedient to all the instructions; now God was going to move. After four months of attending the new church, I was asked to speak to the congregation on a Tuesday night. That twenty-minute message was a preparation for things to come. At the sixth month, I was asked to assist the women's ministry leader. God was moving quickly. As Zechariah 4:10 says:

Do not despise these small beginnings, for the LORD rejoices to see the work begin, to see the plumb line in Zerubbabel's hand. For these seven lamps represent the eyes of the LORD that search all around the world." (NLT)

I waited for the next doors to open.

CHAPTER 32

The Handshake - Betrayal to Promotion

> *But Jesus said to him, "Judas, are you betraying the Son of Man with a kiss?"* Luke 22:48

Judas, one of Jesus' twelve disciples, was the person who kissed Jesus, identifying Him, catapulting Him to the cross, and ultimately sending Him to sit at the right hand of the Father. Although it may be difficult to understand, the kiss had to happen so that Jesus could be established in the place God had assigned Him to. For me, the betrayal came in the form of a handshake. The pastor's handshake played an integral role in the whole process: from a dream, to shaking his hand, to being asked not to shake his hand, which eventually led to my *season of waiting*.

I knew the season was over when the pastor announced that a worldwide healing ministry was saving seats for the congregation at an upcoming event. I had already planned on attending and would be sitting with a friend from the church, but when the announcement was made, I knew this was the time for me to return. Particularly since the announcement was coupled with the fact that the Lord had given me the following scripture:

> *and when the daughter of Herodias herself came in and danced, she pleased Herod and his dinner guests; and the king said to the girl, "Ask me for whatever you want and I will give it to you."* Mark 6:22

Herod was pleased with the young woman's dancing, so he gave her whatever she wanted. With me, I believe the King of kings was saying to me, "I am well-pleased with your obedience. Tell me what you want, and I will give it to you." I wanted to return to the church on my birthday. Unbeknownst to me, the handshake I waited for would be the handshake of betrayal, launching me to another level with the Lord and sending me to a new church.

On the day of the healing crusade, my friend saved me a seat in the church's section at the event. As a commuter, I took the train to and from work, passing through downtown every day, near the location where the event was being held. I got off at the appropriate stop and headed toward the convention center. As I approached the doors, I noticed three men sitting on a bench outside the entrance. Drawing closer, I saw that it was the pastor and two other leaders from the church. As I drew close to the door, the Holy Spirit prompted me to say hello to the men.

Unsure of what to do when they saw me heading toward them, one of the men rose to greet me and invited me to sit in the section assigned for the church. Then the pastor halfway stood up, extended his hand toward me, shook it, and said, "Praise the Lord." I acknowledged the comment, said hello to the other church leader, and headed toward the ballroom. I was in shock that the pastor had extended his hand and shook mine. Eight months earlier, he'd told me never to shake his hand again. The day had arrived when he shook my hand, just as I knew it would.

As I sat waiting for the service to start, many familiar faces greeted me, people saying they were happy to see me. Of course, there were those who were cool toward me, but that was OK. God had shown me at the beginning of the healing process that there were those who were more interested in pleasing the pastor, than pleasing Him. These were the people who were less receptive to my presence. But the most telling reaction was that of the pastor's cousin. When she saw me, her whole face contorted. I had seen that face before – the enemy, not her, was surprised to see me. This was a spiritual battle, not a natural one, and I recognized it as such.

The pastor's father gave me a hug and moved on, but about twenty minutes later, he returned. Knowing the Holy Spirit had directed him to do so, this time I stood up and greeted him again and asked, "May I return to church?" He shrugged his shoulders, as if he didn't know what I was talking about. So, I explained, "I was told I had to be invited back to church," to give him a point of reference for my question.

Again, he shrugged his shoulders and said, "If you want to."

Of course, I did want to return, and said, "I will see you Saturday." With the brief conversation between us over, he walked away.

The betrayal took place upon my return to church.

While riding the train to work one morning during my wait, I praised God, and He gave me a vision. I saw a parade with military personnel standing in formation on both sides of the street. As a convertible with a returning veteran sitting on the backseat passed by, the military personnel gave the veteran both a seven gun salute and a hand salute. I believed the interpretation meant: I was returning to the church and was respected. It turns out my interpretation was inaccurate.

When I entered the church on the evening of my return, the greeting line was full of people on either side, but they were people who weren't normally greeters. Instead, most of the greeters that night were people whose spouses had roles within the church or who served in one of ministries other than the greeting line. At least they hadn't been greeters six months prior to my stepping away. All had somber looks on their faces, except for one gentleman who was not part of the crowd, who was genuinely happy to see me. He and the children told me that they missed me, and their welcome was genuine. It felt like everyone else was just being cordial.

After shaking everyone's hands, I turned the corner to find a seat, only to be met by the pastor and the head usher. The pastor said, "Julie, I thought we agreed that someone from the church would contact you before you returned. You can stay tonight, but you can't come back."

I said, "You shook my hand, and the pastor of the bus ministry invited me to sit with the church group." I didn't mention that his own father had said I could return if I wanted to when we spoke at the healing crusade the Thursday before, because the damage was already done. The pastor responded, "We were only being nice."

I simply replied, "OK" and went to find a seat.

I could have easily been hurt or offended by what transpired, but I wasn't. Offenses will present themselves in all kinds of situations. How we handle the offense determines how God can use us and our destiny in Him. I chose to rise above the situation and move forward.

I sat a moment, taking in the Body of Christ. There were plenty of vacant seats and far fewer people in attendance that Saturday night than had been attending when I left the church. I asked the Lord, "What just happened?" It was the same question I had asked six months prior.

I opened my Bible by faith and received a scripture about treachery. Treachery is defined in the *Merriam-Webster Dictionary* as, "an act of harming someone who trusts you." In that moment, I knew a spirit of treachery existed in that church, and someone I trusted didn't want me there. I needed to stay focused on God, rather than dwell on this revelation or try to determine why I was not welcome. Using an incident like this is exactly how the enemy can operate in the mind, if he is allowed to do so.

While I waited for service to start, Mama saw me. She smiled, extended her hand, and happily greeted me. We didn't speak, however. I still consider her my spiritual mother, even though we haven't seen or talked with each other since that night. I hope the day will come when I can see her again.

As I began to praise and worship, the Lord spoke to me and said, "This will be the last time you are in this church." I knew it to be true, but I needed confirmation. The confirmation came when the pastor issued a call for prayer for those who served or considered themselves members of the church. I had tithed and watched the services online for the past six months, and I still considered myself a member of the church, so I went up for prayer.

The word that proceeded from the pastor's mouth was, "Release."

I had to think about this for a moment, as it was a word of confirmation, though unexpected. Pondering the pastor's comment, I wondered if it was from the Lord. My conclusion was this: whether it was of flesh or of the Lord didn't matter, as God had always used those preaching from the pulpit as a form of confirmation. Trusting Him, I knew this was my last time at the church.

During the service the head usher came up to me and said, "It's really nice seeing you again."

I got closer to him and whispered, "You know the unfortunate part? I won't be back tomorrow. Do you know how many tears I have shed for this church?" He put his head down in resignation and walked away.

His statement was kind and from his heart. The words were like oil being poured on me; just like the woman who broke the alabaster jar and poured the oil on Jesus' head. The story is found in Matthew 26:6-13. At the end of service he escorted me out of the church.

My written confirmation came when I returned home, started to pray, and opened the Word in faith. I received Luke 10:11:

> Even the dust of your city which clings to your feet we wipe off in protest against you; yet be sure of this, that the kingdom of God has come near.

It was the same scripture I had received the last time pastor and I had spoken. Six months earlier, God gave me a choice, and I chose to do God's will, which led to my *season of waiting*; this time, it was an instruction.

This was the last instruction I would receive regarding the pastor. I wiped the dust off of my feet, knowing I was obedient to what God had asked me to do over the last two-and-a-half years. In the early morning, God spoke to me and said, "There are no more opportunities for the pastor." I am unsure of what God meant by the statement, but I know what the statement meant to me. We are all given free will; I believe the pastor chose his will rather than God's, but I will never know for sure. I simply made a decision to move forward.

During my six month absence, not only did I shed tears of healing for myself, but I cried tears of supplication, asking the Lord to have mercy on the church. No one knew but God. On Friday afternoon, as I waited in line for the doors to open for the second day of the healing crusade, a man I knew from church came up to me and said, "Tears of prayer. God has seen the tears you have shed."

The handshake I had waited for led to a different outcome, but it was a promotion, just as the prophetic word in March said it would be.

CHAPTER 33

Suddenly

Then Hezekiah and all the people rejoiced over what God had prepared for the people, because the thing came about suddenly. 2 Chronicles 29:36

God opened the door and I walked through it. My *suddenly* came to pass on my birthday in March, after I had returned to the church the last Saturday of the month for three short hours.

My *season of waiting* was over, and I now had an answer and another instruction. The instruction was to go to the church I had attended only twice before. God said He had a word for me. Being obedient, I went, not knowing what to expect. As the congregation began to praise and worship our Lord and Savior, the Holy Spirit began to move. It's a small church, but the Spirit of the Lord is even stronger in this church than in the church from which I had just been released. The man of God, who moves in a prophetic anointing, began to name aches, pains, and diseases God was healing.

He gave a healing altar call, and due to the heat that was radiating from my hand as we prayed for each other, the woman standing next to me suggested I go up. When the man of God came to me, he asked what part of me needed healing, and I replied, "A bone spur on my foot." He began to pray, but the prayer for healing was just one sentence. He then he broke out in a prophetic word, which was not only a confirmation on many levels, but a release to a new level in my walk with the Lord. The word was:

"Lord Jesus, we thank You, we praise You, we glorify Your Holy name. Lord, right now, Father, in Jesus' name, you have done so much for Julie, you show me. You've done so much, Lord. That is what He is showing me. And He says that He is going to continue to show forth His glory and His power in your life, because you have offered yourself to Him. ... Everything God does is big and grand and great. And He is going to do great things because God wants to show off His power, God wants to show off His greatness. That exceeding greatness of His power that He demonstrated in Christ when He raised Him from the dead and set Him at His own right hand. "Far above all principalities and powers, you will know the greatness of My glory. You will know the greatness of My hand upon your life," sayeth the Lord. "For I am going to make a big splash. ..." God is going to do big things. ... Praise God. God does big things in your life. ... God's healing you of some hurts and stuff, even from Christians in the past and churches. God is bringing you out of all that. Amen. It has been hard to trust people. You have a wall around you, but God says, "I'm bringing down that wall." He's bringing down walls. Amen. ... But God has brought you here, because He is healing you. He says, "You have freedom here to be yourself and just worship Me. Because as you be yourself in Me, I will be Myself in you." Hallelujah. God's going to give you the keys to open doors that no man can shut. The keys to the Kingdom, in Jesus' name. Amen. I say, "YES!" The Man of God says, "She says yes. Yes? Amen. Praise God. God bless you, Julie."

After the word was spoken, I opened my eyes and I saw the man of God looking and smiling at me with a big, beautiful smile. I stood there, not knowing what to make of the incident, and after a few seconds, I returned to my seat. The man of God never preached, but he did talk about serving in the church, and I do remember thinking to myself,

"Maybe now I can be used according to the talents God has given me." I was very excited as I sat on the sidelines and watched for five years at the other church, never being asked to help in a more significant capacity, even though I offered my services on many occasions. Twelve hours after being released from one church, I had a new church home and was ready for all that God had for me.

My *suddenly* took place.

I was open to the change. I was flexible. All I needed was for God to give me the answer and direction, so I could move forward. At first, although I accepted the answer and change, I was in shock. I had to reread the prophetic word about having a husband. If I would "just follow My instructions ... just do it My way," I would have the husband I am supposed to have according to the word. I followed all the instructions, but I believe free will played a role in the outcome. God could have told me to wait longer, but He didn't. He knew the outcome, even though I didn't.

After a few weeks of reflecting on what had transpired, God brought to mind the scripture, Isaiah 55:9:

> "For as the heavens are higher than the earth, So are My ways higher than your ways And My thoughts than your thoughts.

Based on all the spiritual things and the confirmations that took place over the previous two-and-a-half years, I knew the pastor was supposed to be my husband. Now I came to the conclusion that God already knew that he would ultimately reject me as his wife, and He had my destiny all planned.

During the third Sunday service I attended at the new church, I received great revelation about God knowing exactly what was going to happen at the former church. While speaking with a woman during the pot-blessing lunch, the Lord spoke to me and said, "Repent." I knew I had to ask for forgiveness, as my thought of how my life would be was not God's.

Another suddenly occurred when I had a revelation about following the instructions and doing things His way. I truly understood Isaiah 55:9. I could loosely make my plans, but I had to trust God with fulfilling them according to His will. For the first time, I understood that other people's decisions can impact how God instructs me with my walk. I heard it best on a Christian television program when the preacher made reference to returning to Plan A because the parties involved in Plan B hadn't done God's will, but their own.

My *suddenly* came as God had showed me six months earlier, according to the scripture. Now I found myself waiting again. God's next move would be significant, and there were still five irons in the fire, five potential doors to open. They were retirement, a new job, ministry, my book and a husband, or any combination of the aforementioned. I knew the open door or doors were close, but everything is in God's time, not ours.

CHAPTER 34

Spiritual Reality

During the healing crusade, God opened doors that no man could shut. This was confirmation of a prophetic word that the California pastor had spoken over me three weeks prior. Part of the prophetic word was:

I see gold. I see gold. Gold is being put into your hands. Trust. I hear trust. I don't know if that means a trust or a trust account or a trust that God is entrusting to you. That's it. He's entrusting to you a trust. ...

Only God could have orchestrated the following chain of events over the two-day crusade.

The friend who was sitting next to me at the healing crusade turned to me and said, "I have been asked to count the offering and they need two more people. Do you want to count the offering with me? They say we will be blessed for doing so."

I replied, "Sure." She asked another woman to join us, so the three of us headed toward the closed door to a room where approximately seven other people were counting the offering that had just been collected.

I walked to the head table, took a seat next to the man from the healing ministry who was in charge of counting the offering, and began to open envelopes, per this man's instructions. As I opened the envelopes, the Lord spoke the words "gold chip." I repeated this to my friend, as she had heard the word spoken over me at the women's ministry meeting.

Then He spoke, "Trust." I did not share this word, as I knew God was showing me something. He was entrusting me with His money.

The two women left, but I stayed behind because I knew there was a reason I was counting the money. I commented to the man from the ministry about the word *trust* and he just looked at me with big eyes and a huge smile. When I had finished my job and was ready to leave, the man prayed over me that whatever God was entrusting to me would come to fruition, or something on that order.

The service was almost over by the time I returned to my seat. I left the event, headed to the train stop, and waited for the light rail to arrive. As I waited, a divine appointment occurred. A woman waiting alongside me struck up a conversation. I shared with her about counting the ministry's money, and she told me something very profound. She explained to me how only the high priest in the Old Testament was given the responsibility to count the offering of the Temple.

All of a sudden, the following scripture I had been receiving for the past few weeks made sense:

> When they saw that there was much money in the chest, the king's scribe and the high priest came up and tied it in bags and counted the money which was found in the house of the LORD. They gave the money which was weighed out into the hands of those who did the work, who had the oversight of the house of the LORD; and they paid it out to the carpenters and the builders who worked on the house of the LORD;
> 2 Kings 12:10-11

God was entrusting me with His money – my paycheck or unexpected money that comes my way is all His. It is my responsibility to be a good steward of it. Whether it is my tithe or giving someone money to help them out, I have been obedient to God's Word and directions. God was showing me that He could trust me with His money as He instructed. Spiritually, I am His high priest, in whom He trusts. I knew this revelation was for now and for the future.

The next day, I took my seat at the crusade and listened to the message. Every once in a while, I glanced over at the pastor, only to find him glancing at me. This occurred over the course of both nights. At the end of the service, the healing pastor made an altar call for a fresh anointing. I went up to the front and stood with my hands held high. In the Spirit, I saw a beam of light coming down into the palms of my hands. At the time, I didn't understand what God was doing, but knew it was something important.

After the fresh anointing was released, my eyes met those of the healing pastor. I looked at him and he looked at me, but when he looked at me, it was as if God was speaking to him, telling him something about me. His eyebrows raised, but he remained composed. He told the congregation that he had tried to hold the March crusade in other cities, but they hadn't worked out, and Phoenix kept coming into the picture.

I knew God had ordained these two days so I could return to church. The spiritual reality that God had orchestrated the whole event for the pastor and me was mind boggling. Events like the men from the church leadership sitting outside the venue when I arrived, Pastor's father talking to me, and counting the offering on Thursday night showed me how much He loves me and is willing to battle on my behalf. That's not to say I was the only one for whom God had plans. Everyone at the crusade was predestined to be there for their respective reasons, whether for a healing, a word, or a friendship, God had it all planned.

As I left the event, I ran into an acquaintance from the church. We exchanged phone numbers and a friendship was established. I told her I would be returning to church tomorrow, Saturday. Although my return at the old church was short lived, my promotion took place the next day when I landed at a new church. It was there that my daily experiences in the spirit over the past two-and-a-half years were given a name: *spiritual reality*. The man of God at the new church spent the next few weeks teaching on spiritual reality. I completely understood the term and the messages, as I was walking it.

CHAPTER 35

Understanding the Call to Ministry

The pastor closed the door for my future attendance at the church, but I stayed that evening. I happened to sit next to a blind man as I took my seat and across from a married couple, who were mutual acquaintances. Those three people were instrumental in God placing me on the path toward my destiny. God turned around an unfortunate situation for His good and glory. The pastor had given an altar call, telling the people to line up so he could pray for each one. The blind man and I sat on the aisle and watched as people walked past us to line up. A few individuals asked the man if he needed assistance going up for the pastor's call. He graciously declined them all, but when I told him I would be happy to lead him, he agreed.

We chatted as we walked up the aisle, arm in arm. We walked up the steps and stood so the pastor could pray for us. Upon returning to our seats, I saw the woman I had talked to briefly before the service looking at me. I asked her if she wanted to tell me something. She paused, and her husband came out into the aisle where I was standing and said, "I shouldn't be doing this, but the Lord has shown us something about you, and I need to anoint and pray for you."

He began to speak a word so profound, I asked him to write it down afterwards. One thing about being in the Spirit and speaking prophetically: the person speaking often doesn't remember a lot of what he or she said, and neither does the recipient. That was certainly true in this case. All I remember is that he anointed my forehead and said:

As you led the blind man across the podium, God showed us you are a leader to the blind. Veils will be removed from believers, so they can see the truth. At the same time, for those who don't know Jesus, their veil would be removed, so that they will come into a personal relationship with Him...

His word went on in this vein for several minutes, and I knew it to be true.

What took place in the spiritual over the past several months of my life away from the church was now displayed in the natural. God was giving me a specific mission and ministry which were now being revealed, so I had a better understanding. The man wrote the following:

Hold yourself accountable to the Father. He is calling you as a leader of the blind and will open your understanding of Jesus. Everything will come from your personal relationship with Him.

At the top of the paper he wrote Ephesians 1:18, which says:

I pray that the eyes of your heart may be enlightened, so that you will know what is the hope of His calling, what are the riches of the glory of His inheritance in the saints,

As I *walk out* the call God has placed on my life, the ministry is beginning to be revealed. Although I don't have a complete understanding of it yet, He has shown me that the personal experiences I explain in this book are catalysts for the *blind* to see. The testimonies, processes, lessons learned, and revelations are trumpets of His voice sounding out to believers and nonbelievers alike. Many people attend church but do not understand God and how He moves in each of our lives. I believe He has called me to help others come to a greater understanding and into the fullness of their own destiny, ultimately leading to a deeper personal relationship with Him. At the same time, the ministry will bring an awareness and understanding of the Father, Son, and Holy Spirit for the nonbeliever, and bring him or her into the Kingdom of God and their predestined purpose.

A few months after I left the church, I was looking for a specific business card in my wallet. As I searched for it, my business card with this couple's phone number written on the back fell out. I called immediately, and the woman and I talked for about fifteen minutes. I explained to her what God was doing in my life since I had left the church, telling her I was receiving deeper revelation about becoming a leader to the blind and the beginning of the ministry.

She got goose bumps, which was a confirmation to me of what God was about to do in my life. Although short-lived, my three-hour return to the church was a pivotal point in my life, as the ministry to which I received a call that night began to unfold over the next several months.

CHAPTER 36
God's Will vs. Free Will

God will never force Himself upon us. From the beginning of creation, God has given us instructions, but we have the choice to follow them or not. As Genesis 2:16-17 says:

> The LORD God commanded the man, saying, "From any tree of the garden you may eat freely; but from the tree of the knowledge of good and evil you shall not eat, for in the day that you eat from it you will surely die."

God gave the instruction to Adam, but Adam did not follow it. Whether we chose to follow the instructions or not will determine our destiny. In the case of the pastor, I do not know if God gave him any instructions to follow related to me, but I followed His instructions, and eventually God closed the door for me at that church. A year from the time his father prophesied that the pastor would be joined by his beautiful wife on the pulpit, the pastor wasn't married, and I was no longer a member.

God will give us many opportunities to get it right, yet if we continually walk outside of His will for us, consequences will come. I saw it happen with my ex-husband, and I heard what happened with the pastor. Not only did his church attendance decrease, but for a season he was sick. When I learned he was in the hospital for surgery, my prayer was that he ask God to show him what he needed to do to get it right, repent, and then follow God's instructions for him.

About eight weeks after I left the church, I heard that the message he preached upon his return from his illness was about holding your tongue. I believe had he waited on the Lord and followed the instructions he might be married, attendance at his church might be increasing, and God would have used us in a powerful way for His glory.

I shared the spiritual reality of my return to the church with someone who didn't know me or the entire situation. On hearing the story, the person said, "It's not that he didn't see the spiritual reality of what God was doing. It was the power God has instilled in you that gripped him with fear." I had never thought of his non-response as one of fear. God told me I was going to do greater work than my husband. Perhaps his pride got in the way, as he wanted to be the one in the limelight? I will never know why it happened. I followed God's commands, and I moved forward.

I learned "God's will vs. free will" the hard way with a terrible marriage. During my childhood, I always did what my parents asked. The Ten Commandments are first introduced in Exodus. Specifically, Exodus 20:12 says:

"Honor your father and your mother, that your days may be prolonged in the land which the LORD your God gives you.

Honoring your mother and father is the one commandment with a promise attached to it. I believe that because I usually did what my parents asked me to do and followed their guidance, my life overall was in God's will. I experienced no repercussions due to bad decisions or failing to follow the instructions, other than my marriage.

In the case with the husband I believe God called for me, there is nothing I can do. Ultimately, God knew how he would respond – through his actions and words. God created a helpmate for Adam to oversee God's creation. I believe I was supposed to be the pastor's helpmate for the growth of the church.

I followed all the instructions, and it cost me my membership in the church. But I know I did what God asked of me, whether others liked or believed it, or not. And I report to God, not to any man. Our free will can lead us into a place which God never intended. We have to remember that God only has our best interest at heart and would never place us in a bad situation or give us anything we cannot handle. Deuteronomy 31:8 says:

> The LORD is the one who goes ahead of you; He will be with you. He will not fail you or forsake you. Do not fear or be dismayed.

Knowing this is God's promise, we can trust He will give us the perfect spouse, but we must be willing to follow His instructions and do His will. If we get off track, He is faithful to get us back on track.

Do not think the tough instructions are given immediately. Following the small, simple instructions is where it begins. I remember the very first instruction I received. I was to do a cartwheel in my living room. I was a cheerleader in the seventh grade, but how I got the position was nothing more than the favor of God. Now, I was receiving an instruction to do something that I hadn't been able to do as a cheerleader, nor when I was first born again. It took a few tries, but with God prompting me to continue my efforts, I was able to do one, then two, and soon a few more cartwheels. I knew at that moment I was hearing His voice.

Next, He instructed me to go to the grocery store across the street and wait in the cafeteria. I waited for what seemed liked forever, but within about twenty minutes, five guys from Ireland walked in and sat down beside me. We struck up a conversation, and I noticed that one of them had a badly hurt hand. The Lord spoke and said, "Pray for his healing." I asked if I could pray for his hand and he agreed, so I took it in mine, prayed out loud, and walked out a few minutes later. I had heard the instruction and followed God's will.

Over the years, the instructions became tougher; the most difficult ones are mentioned in this book. The point is this: do His will and follow

His instructions, as they are directly related to your destiny. I heard that membership was decreasing at the pastor's church. Evidently, shortly after I was asked to leave, the pastor told the congregation that it was God's church and if He was removing people from the church, that was His will. But whether the drop in attendance was due to willful disobedience or something else, I do not know.

Two of the best known examples of willful disobedience to the Lord are Moses and King Saul. Moses was unable to go into the Promised Land because he did not believe God.

> But the LORD said to Moses and Aaron, "Because you have not believed Me, to treat Me as holy in the sight of the sons of Israel, therefore you shall not bring this assembly into the land which I have given them." Numbers 20:12

Further, it states in Deuteronomy 34:4:

> Then the LORD said to him, "This is the land which I swore to Abraham, Isaac, and Jacob, saying, 'I will give it to your descendants'; I have let you see it with your eyes, but you shall not go over there."

God allowed Moses to see the Promised Land, but he was unable to enter.

1 Samuel 15 recounts how God gave King Saul instructions, but King Saul lost his kingship because of his disobedience. As 1 Samuel 15:10-11 says:

> Then the word of the LORD came to Samuel, saying, "I regret that I have made Saul king, for he has turned back from following Me and has not carried out My commands." And Samuel was distressed and cried out to the LORD all night.

Verse 35, the last verse of the chapter, explains King Saul's final outcome, saying:

> Samuel did not see Saul again until the day of his death; for Samuel grieved over Saul. And the LORD regretted that He had made Saul king over Israel.

For me, God had provided a new church. Additionally, incredible prophetic words were being spoken over me by different people, all with the same theme: "big things" and "it's getting ready to start." I was obedient to the instructions and my obedience was now bearing fruit. I now understood the prophetic words spoken over me by the California Pastor that dealt with David. A small part of a larger word, these specific words were:

> But the Lord says, "I'm building the house. I'm establishing My covenant with you. The sure mercies of David, the House of David, the lineage of David, the covenant of God is with you."

I believe God gave the pastor two years to get it right, but the time came when the opportunities stopped. At that point, the destiny changed for each of us, based on how we followed the Lord's instructions. He will still use each of us. And I only know what God was telling me to do. A friend said it best: "If the pastor doesn't do what God has asked of him, then another man will come along and the ministry that the two of you will have will be even bigger than what was originally planned." I received that word. Almost a year later, the Lord spoke to me and said, "the book first, then the husband."

Understanding God's will for our lives and doing it can be difficult. Our human nature wants to do things our way, based on the information available. God knows all things, so we need to trust that He knows what is best for us and gives us instructions accordingly, even if they seem strange. I asked for confirmation on numerous occasions, and He always confirmed His instructions. On the rare occasions that I didn't ask for confirmation, I would temporarily be out of His will, but grace abounds at all times.

Being able to live according to God's will was easy in the beginning of my walk with the Lord. He gave me an instruction to move, so I moved. He gave me an instruction to start a business, I did. It was when I walked away from God's will by marrying my husband that my life became challenging. When I earnestly sought God's face by reading the Word, praying, and singing worship songs, it became easier to let Him lead.

Listen to the instructions, follow them, and watch God move in your life. Do His will, as He wants only the best for you; even when it doesn't seem like it. Your destiny depends on cooperating with the Lord. Make wise decisions by seeking God's face, asking for counsel when appropriate, and stepping out in faith by following the instructions you receive.

CHAPTER 37
Forgiveness

In the ultimate act of forgiveness, Jesus died on the cross for each one of us. Matthew 27 details the crucifixion, death, and burial of Jesus. Luke 23:34 states:

> But Jesus was saying, "Father, forgive them; for they do not know what they are doing." And they cast lots, dividing up His garments among themselves.

Often, when someone offends us or we offend others, humans harbor the offense, whether it's a comment or action that causes us pain. Through all the misunderstandings, hurtful comments, and rude actions I experienced, it would have been understandable if I had become angry or bitter, harbored resentment, or left the church – but I didn't do any of those.

The longer I walk with Jesus, the more Christ-like I become. This is not a prideful statement, but a statement of confidence about who I am in Christ. Paul says in Galatians 6:14:

> But may it never be that I would boast, except in the cross of our Lord Jesus Christ, through which the world has been crucified to me, and I to the world.

Forgiveness is very easy for me, and forgiving the pastor, the leadership, or the Body of Christ was no exception. Luke 17:4 says:

And if he sins against you seven times a day, and returns to you seven times, saying, 'I repent,' forgive him.

I understood the leadership's thought processes. They wanted only the best for the pastor and to protect him. I suspect there had been a few crazy women who had approached the pastor for whatever reason, so their response was actually understandable. The pastor would say every once in a while, "If it's a duck, it will quack, just give it some time." Perhaps they thought my instructions were not of God, but He always vindicated me from the pulpit, so they should have known my actions were at God's direction.

I said to mama, "It was an instruction," when she looked at me quizzically as I handed her the draft book. Though it may have seemed like a quack, it was not.

I forgave them immediately, and as the Holy Spirit would show me things to pray for, I hoped in due time that they would understand. But I also needed to ask for forgiveness. Although my actions were ordained by God, the pastor and church leaders didn't know this, so I needed to ask God to forgive me for offending them. I never acted with the intention of offending; that is to say, I didn't act or say anything to deliberately upset anyone.

Some in the congregation were offended by my actions (i.e., the notes), but I believe these people were more concerned about their status with the pastor than they were for his welfare; nevertheless, they sided with him. I don't know if the pastor was aware of it, but people were beginning to shun me. When he preached *Put Down the Rock* from the pulpit, he said, "I need to be wary of those people who always tell me what I want to hear, not what I need to hear." I think pastor may have a lot of people who tell him what they think he wants to hear in order to remain in his inner circle.

For me, it is easier to forgive or ask for forgiveness of people I know, than asking a complete stranger to forgive me or apologize to them. I spoke with a sharp tongue for many years, sometimes finding myself saying something offensive when it wasn't meant to be. I would then have to turn and apologize to the person. Saying you're sorry to someone you don't know is a very humbling experience.

One such occasion comes to my mind. I arrived at church early and had placed my Bible on a chair before the service to save my seat. When I returned, I found a purse on the chair. I asked the woman sitting in the chair next to the purse if it was hers, and she said, "Yes."

I pointed to the seat and asserted, "This is *my* chair." She made no attempt to move her purse, and I became agitated, as if I owned the chair. I made another comment, and she moved her purse.

As the praise and worship portion of the service began, the Holy Spirit convicted me of my words and actions. I had to apologize. I gulped, turned to the woman, and said, "I'm sorry for my rude behavior." She gave me a hug and accepted the apology. We became friends after that incident. Whenever I saw her and her granddaughter at church, I made a point of talking to them. She attended the church for a season, maybe six months. When I hadn't seen her for a while, I asked around and learned she had moved back to Detroit. I still think about her every so often.

In February, a well-known female teacher came to Phoenix, as she does every year. A friend drove in from Show Low to attend the conference and asked if I wanted to join her. I said, "Sure." Over the three days of the conference, the speaker taught about offenses: offenses to others, offenses to oneself, and offenses toward God. After each session, I cried without knowing why. Even my girlfriend thought it was strange. It wasn't until I went to church on Sunday that I had an understanding of what was taking place.

Earlier in the month, I had given the pastor the first note. Everything that God was doing between us just took a different direction. He was angry with me, and I tried to make amends by saying, "I'm sorry. I'm sorry." But, it wasn't until the Sunday after the conference that I understood why I was crying. Not only had I offended the pastor, but I had offended his father, too.

Papa almost always approached me to shake my hand or give me a welcoming hug. Now, I sensed he was avoiding me before the services. I would approach to give him a hug, but he was standoffish. I was shocked and asked, "Have I offended you in some way?" He sheepishly shrugged his shoulders. I asked if it was because of the note I had given to his son, and he nodded yes. I couldn't believe it. I knew the pastor was upset, but I had no idea his dad, and perhaps his mom, was upset with me as well. Quickly, I apologized and said, "I am so sorry." At home I prayed.

Shortly thereafter, the pastor preached on offenses. Sometimes the recipient of the offense needs *to get over it*. The receiver needs to forgive the messenger of the offense and ask God to forgive themselves for being offended. As Proverbs 19:11 states:

> A man's wisdom gives him patience; it is to his glory to overlook an offense. (NIV)

In another translation, the *New American Standard* says:

> A man's discretion makes him slow to anger, And it is his glory to overlook a transgression.

The pastor talked about forgiveness as a weapon. He said, "When we hold on to unforgiveness, it's like a cancer that spreads over time and it steals our destiny. It steals our assignment, it steals our future, it steals our greatness, it steals the power of God in our lives, and it paralyzes us from moving forward and accomplishing the greatness that God has called us to. It will take us out. It keeps us hostage to the past and steals our future. Let it go."

> "Do not judge, and you will not be judged. Do not condemn, and you will not be condemned. Forgive, and you will be forgiven. Luke 6:37 (NIV)

It is so much easier to forgive than harbor sentiments of anger or hurt. The only person who is hurt is the one who can't or won't forgive. With the exception of the bitterness that tried to creep into my life months after I was asked to leave the church, I have always been quick to forgive.

I have heard of instances of people being very sick, yet once they forgave the person who had offended them, their health improved or they were healed. I decided to research this hypothesis and found many articles on the Internet that directly correlated unforgiveness with health issues. Besides the occasional headache or common cold, I have never been sick. Maybe it is due to the ease of forgiving others who have offended me, and asking God to forgive them as well. Usually my prayer is something like this, "Lord, please forgive *so and so* for saying what they said or did to me. They didn't know I was offended. I forgive them of their words or actions, and I ask You forgive them, as well."

In the same manner, asking forgiveness for offending others is just as important. In such a case, my prayer is something like this, "Lord, please forgive me for offending *so and so* with my words or actions. Help me to not offend the person again, In Jesus name I pray."

One never knows if the other person realizes you were offended, so it is better to ask on their behalf. If you can, talk to the person and clear the air. In my case, I would have loved to talk with the pastor, but since I was asked not to contact him or return to the church, I honored their request. Maybe one day the Lord will open the door for us to talk and set things straight between us. I never closed the door, and I forgave all parties involved with regard to my experiences. Yes, it was uncomfortable at times, but I was doing God's will, and I knew it. I was put to the test of forgiving others, and my inner self was strengthened at the same time. The enemy would have liked nothing more than for me to speak poorly about the pastor or the church leadership, but I never did.

The last thing the pastor said from the pulpit as he pointed at me that fateful Saturday night is found in Isaiah 54:17:

> "No weapon that is formed against you will prosper; And every

tongue that accuses you in judgment you will condemn. This is the heritage of the servants of the LORD, and their vindication is from Me," declares the LORD.

I just looked at him and thought, "Really?" I forgave him for that statement, too.

I knew he was referring to the book. Based on everything I experienced and have shared in this book, I believed the pastor was supposed to be my husband, so why would I do anything against him? I believe this testimony, in which he has an important role, will serve the purpose that God intends. This book is not about him or me; it is about the Father, Son, and Holy Spirit. It is about understanding how God works in our lives to bring us into our destiny, forgiveness, and salvation through Jesus Christ, the One True Husband.

Like the toothpaste analogy, we need to think about our words and actions before they happen, as once said or done, they are impossible to take back. To move forward, ask for forgiveness, forgive the offender, or both.

CHAPTER 38
The Personal Allegory

As I waited for the ending of the book, for my husband to come, God gave me the revelation in the midnight hour that the book was an allegory, a story with a hidden meaning, but this story was personal. Just as I continue to wait for my husband, so does the church, the Body of Christ, wait for the return of Jesus, her Husband.

During the wait, God has taken me through processes, lessons, revelations, and repentance. The discipline, healing, and instructions all serve a specific purpose. He continues to draw me closer to Him. He has healed me of past hurts, shown me more about who He is and how much He loves me and all of us. Life is a journey, a process, and how well I listen to the instructions and am obedient to Him determines my destiny. Life happens – the good, the bad, and the ugly. The way I handle each situation draws me closer to the plan God has for me. The same goes for the church.

> *For I know the plans I have for you," declares the LORD, "plans to prosper you and not to harm you, plans to give you hope and a future.* Jeremiah 29:11 (NIV)

I believe the instructions I followed confirmed that the Pastor was my husband, so I waited for him. Jesus teaches the same concept. He brings people into our lives who follow the instruction to share His love, the good news of Yeshua, and He confirms it. Paul said in 1 Corinthians 3:6-7:

> *I planted, Apollos watered, but God gave the increase. So then neither he who plants is anything, nor he who waters, but God who gives the increase.* (NKJV)

God confirms His love to the world and His desire that we come unto Him by using people to *plant* and/or *water* individuals' lives. Whether it be sharing a personal testimony, an appropriate scripture, or praying for someone, He is always knocking on our heart, hoping we will be open to Him and His perfect will for each of us.

> *Jesus said to him, "I am the way, and the truth, and the life; no one comes to the Father but through Me.* John 14:6

But God is gracious and He will never force Himself on us. The pastor had a choice to accept me as his wife, or not; and so it is with Jesus. We have the choice and free will to decide whether we want to accept Him as our husband, our Lord and Savior, or not. The Pastor ultimately said no to me, but Jesus never says no to anyone.

> *The Lord is not slow about His promise, as some count slowness, but is patient toward you, not wishing for any to perish but for all to come to repentance.* 2 Peter 3:9

As I wait for my earthly husband to come and sweep me off my feet, I take care of myself – I eat healthy food, exercise, and have personal care time (e.g., haircuts, facials, and reflexology). Only God knows when my chosen partner will come to me. As I wait for my Heavenly Husband, I prepare myself by reading the Word of God, praying, and worshipping through song. When He will come for me, only God knows.

As the prophet once said to me, "Any man would be honored to have you as his wife." And so it is with Jesus, He is honored to have each one of us as His bride.

CHAPTER 39

Reflections

I continue on the road before me, I pray that I walk in joy, peace, patience, kindness, goodness, faithfulness, gentleness, and self-control – the fruits of the Spirit – at all times. We all have good treasure and prosperity in Him. Prosperity is living secure in who you are as a child of God, knowing that He is with you at all times. It is knowing that you can trust the promises written in the Bible and trust Jesus when he said:

> ... I came that they may have life, and have it abundantly.
> John 10:10

He wants to heal us of our physical, spiritual, emotional, and psychological hurts. He wants each of us to live with joy:

> for the kingdom of God is not a matter of eating and drinking, but of righteousness, peace and joy in the Holy Spirit.
> Romans 14:17

He wants to bless us, as Deuteronomy 28:1-14 explains. He is our strong Fortress, Deliverer, Jehovah Jireh (God who Provides), Jehovah Roffe (God who Heals), Prince of Peace, Love, Peace, Merciful, Kind, and He is Good. The list goes on and on – whatever you need Him to be in that moment in time, He is. Just stand on His promises.

This personal allegory is a snapshot of what God has done in my life. I share with candor and transparency the events I experienced, knowing I followed His instructions. I had to repent of self-deprecation, as I would say to the Lord, "Who wants to read what I write?"

He answered, "Just write."

He knows the purpose of this book, and I have learned not to interject my own expectations or limitations on how He is using me. I hope people will gain insight into how God works in each of our lives. Every person's destiny is different, and we can't compare our lives to one another, although there may be similarities. We are each created uniquely, with a specific purpose to fulfill. Don't place God in a box or get religious, for it is a personal relationship we each have with Jesus. Romans 8:28 says:

> And we know that God causes all things to work together for good to those who love God, to those who are called according to His purpose.

I wouldn't change anything about my walk with the Lord or the process God brought me through in order for me to be in His perfect will. Sure, it was difficult at times, and I shed a lot of tears, but my husband will be one of my many rewards for doing God's will and not my own. And then my reward in heaven awaits me – eternal life.

What an incredible life God has given to each one of us, if we will just walk in it.

CHAPTER 40
Salvation

Will you make Jesus, the Lord and Savior of your life?

Algun Dia es Hoy! Translated from Spanish to English, this means, "Someday is today." Have you said to yourself, "Yeah, *someday* I will ask Jesus to come into my life and be my Lord and Savior"? Well, **someday is TODAY.** Remember, it is never too late with Jesus, and no sin or past is too serious for Him to forgive. Pray this prayer:

> *Lord God, I have sinned and fallen short of Your glory. Redeem me of my sins, as I ask for Jesus to come into my heart to make me the whole person You have called me to be. I confess with my mouth and believe in my heart that Jesus died on the cross for me. I believe that Jesus is the Son of the Living God. Holy Spirit, be my Helper as I start my new life in Christ. As I meditate on Your Word, keep me on the path that you have for me. Psalm 119:105 says, "Your word is a lamp to my feet and a light to my path." I will trust you for all things, as only You have my best interest at heart. Thank you that Your loving kindness is from everlasting to everlasting. In Jesus name I pray. Amen (so it is).*

Now that you have prayed the prayer of salvation, your sins are in the past, no longer to be counted against you. Begin to read the Bible, the Word of God. When I was first saved, the person who led me to the Lord told me the following, "Before you begin reading, ask God to give you wisdom (God's greatest gift, as explained in Proverbs, chapters

1-4), knowledge, and understanding. For Exodus 31:3 says:

> *"I have filled him with the Spirit of God in wisdom, in understanding, in knowledge, and in all kinds of craftsmanship,*

If you don't understand what you are reading, start by reading the books of Psalms or Proverbs. Let God begin to move in you. You will start to see a transformation, and it will not be by your will that the "new you" is born; it's through the Living Word.

> *For the word of God is living and active and sharper than any two-edged sword, and piercing as far as the division of soul and spirit, of both joints and marrow, and able to judge the thoughts and intentions of the heart.* Hebrews 4:12

Start to talk (pray) to God in the name of Jesus, as He intercedes on your behalf to the Father. Ask according to (in alignment with) the Word of God. As John 16:23 says:

> *"In that day you will not question Me about anything. Truly, truly, I say to you, if you ask the Father for anything in My name, He will give it to you.*

Be honest with Him, as He already knows your heart and motives. He knows what you need and what He has planned for you.

My prayer for you is that this book has ministered to you in a special way that only you and God know. I pray that as God begins to move in your life, you will experience the fullness He has ordained for you from the beginning of time. May you rejoice in the times of trials and tribulations and give Him praise in good times and bad. May He give you the desires of your heart, according to His perfect will.

The LORD bless you, and keep you; the LORD make His face shine on you, and be gracious to you; the LORD lift up His countenance on you, And give you peace.' Numbers 6:24-26

And finally, may you come into the revelation of how to live *On Earth as It Is in Heaven.*

Acknowledgements

A heartfelt thank you goes to each person who planted a seed of support during my twenty-nine year journey.

Suzanne Myal, my mom, who established Fiesta Publishing more than 20 years ago. Without her invaluable knowledge of book publishing and assistance with research, everything would have taken much longer. Her unconditional love and support as I pursue my destiny is immeasurable and without her I would not be the woman I am today.

Mick Myal, my dad, who passed away in 2012, who imparted into me how to write concisely over the course of 30 years. He was the founder, editor and publisher of Contact! Magazine, and gave me the opportunity to transcribe interviews and proofread articles for the first 13 years of publication. At the time, I had no idea what was in store for me, I was just helping out my dad.

I am so glad that God called you, Mick and Sue, to be my parents.

Laura Orsini, editor and word smith, whose gift for words helped make this book the trumpet God called it to be. Words are powerful and your talent makes this book living and active.

Lucy C. Flores, whose God-given understanding and vision for the cover explains the book visually – the steps I climbed to reach the open door.

Kristi Church, Alli Masi and the team at Infinite Reach Agency: Your generosity and faith in this book takes on a whole new meaning when the scripture says, you reap what you sow (2 Corinthians 9:6). Thank you for believing in me, Fiesta Publishing and the book.

Bryon Keck, your easygoing approach to creating Fiesta Publishing's website and featuring *On Earth as It Is in Heaven, a Personal Allegory* was a blessing. You created a website that will be used for God's glory.

Ebony, Deb R., Marianne, Deb G., Rose, Whitney, Tamera, Kathy, Anita, Valerie K., Laura, Nancy, Vicki and Barbara: Thank you for your words of encouragement and your support as God unfolded my journey. God used each of you in your respective way as I wrote the book.

Pastors Patrick and Eddie, and Christine: Thank you for the prophetic words that served as confirmations for the book, embracing me at church, your obedience and recognizing God's plan and destiny for me.

And finally, Mac, my son, who has been with me throughout the journey, the good, the bad and the ugly; but who never said a discouraging word, only wishing me joy and happiness in my pursuit of God's will. I pray that as you continue in your pursuit of knowledge that God's hand will continually be with you. That you will experience the desires of your heart and come into the fullness of your destiny.

About the Author

It was inevitable Julie Castro would write and publish a book. Her mom wrote and self-published two travel guidebooks, while her dad founded, edited, and published Contact! Magazine. Julie assisted both her parents with editing, transcription, and even the fun of eating Mexican food while researching her mother's book, *Tucson's Mexican Restaurants*. Grant writing also became a talent, as she was awarded several grants while she was serving as director of a completely grant-funded community outreach program.

Julie's writing skills continued to develop as she was responsible for all workforce related proposals and documents for several of the Governor's advisory councils and commissions. An article she wrote for the National Council of University Research Administrators (NCURA), *It's All in the Asking*, was published in the March/April 2013 magazine.

Having a personal relationship with Jesus for 29 years, Julie has lived her life according to His will, leading her to new cities, jobs, churches, and the understanding of walking heaven on earth. She finds living in the Lord an adventure and never knows where she will be led to go or who she will encounter each day. She currently resides in Phoenix with her son's cat, Saki.

www.ingramcontent.com/pod-product-compliance
Lightning Source LLC
Chambersburg PA
CBHW050631300426
44112CB00012B/1745